ESSAYS

IN COUNSELLING & PSYCHOTHERAPY

BY ALEX H PARKER

Copyright © 2012 by Alex H Parker.

Published by Alex H Parker.co.uk & Plessey Castle.

All rights reserved. Printed in Great Britain. No part of this book may be used in any manner whatsoever without written permission except in the case of brief quotations embodied in critical articles or academic work.

Contents of paperback version:

Gestalt Therapy 7

Loss and Grief 14

Transactional Analysis with Humanistic perspective................19

Relationship therapy 25

Humanistic perspective..31

Disabilities and self actualisation..36

Cultural Counselling..41

Stress Counselling..49

Psychoanalysis. 54

Personal Development Statement: Transference...................60

Personal Development Statement: Gestalt............................62

Personal Development: Statement in Time of Crisis...................64

Personal Development: Automatic thoughts..........................67

Final Personal development Statement. 70

Introduction

As an adult, writing essays can be a nightmare especially if you have not been accustomed to writing anything since your school days. I personally was one of those students who would receive his work back from the teacher covered in red pen, pointing out the grammatical and spelling mistakes. Nothing much has changed, but at least I have a chance as an adult to write some essays using word processing programs like MS Word. Like many adults returning to college I was daunted by the prospect of being evaluated by a teacher and was reminded of the humiliation I would experience every-time I had my work handed back to me with a big 'F' in red pen at the bottom of the page. In the 21st century the computer appears to be able to assist almost everyone to write something that is decipherable. I have a bit of a love/hate relationship with my laptop. I need to keep reminding myself that when it underlines my errors with a green or red line that it is as a result of its programming and that it's nothing personal; this doesn't stop me using my fingers to sign obscenities at the screen as if it's my old teacher from year 3. I was taught to read using an experimental method of teaching called Initial Teaching Alphabet which taught children how to spell using an alphabet that had about as much use to a child's development as the Star Trek language of Klingon. From the age of three I advanced very quickly using this experimental form of spelling and reading to the point that I became fluent in a language that no one would ever understand. My bubble was burst at the age of seven when I was introduced to normal reading and writing and was suddenly at the bottom of the class with the rest of the ITA students for the rest of our school career. Reading improved by the time I was eleven due to 'The Eagle Comic', I was motivated by my need to understand why 'Doomlord' was killing people and taking their identities. I took an interest in all things space or spiritual. Fortunately my dad would have random books delivered to him from 'Readers Digest' which he would buy in the hope that it would increase his chances of winning their prize draw. Three of these books contained information about alien abductions, local ghost stories and explanations of the solar system. I persisted on reading them over and over again until I got an understanding of their content. The result was that I very quickly became a fluent reader. The difficulty was that my spelling and grammar stayed pretty much as abysmal as it had been before. This was a severe disadvantage as it is accepted that if you can't write very well that your reading must also be of a low standard. By the time I was thirteen I had taken an interest in things of an Occult, Spiritual and scientific nature. I was very much into divination and had acquired a great deal of information from books regarding the subject; I would read like a hermit in my bedroom. At school the class was asked to write about a personal interest. Some students wrote about their interest in football, others about their interest in music. I decided to write about my interest in the occult and with pencil in hand recorded my knowledge in pencil onto forty pieces of A5 paper and even gave it a book cover with a picture of a

Pentagram on the front. The teacher was obviously torn between the emotion of joy at witnessing such a good effort and disgust at my conceit at attempting to write a book with my standard of writing. After complementing my work in front of the class she then expressed her true opinion of my abilities by picking up one of the books I used to reference my work, flicking through to a random page. She then asked me to explain 'The Kabbalah.' Although it was not a favourite subject of mine I was able to recite the definition from the first paragraph and explained that it is a philosophy based on Jewish mysticism. She didn't look impressed and just closed the book and handed it back to me. I am still not sure what that means but at least I was able to give an answer and avoided exposure as a fraud. Later when I was twenty-two I was in my second year of working for Proctor and Gamble making Old Spice aftershave and Pantene hair products I encountered intellectual arrogance of a far higher standard. By this time I had no self confidence left and accepted in my own mind that I lacked intelligence. I was about to encounter my new manager. She was a young university graduate who worshipped education and despised what she saw as ignorance. She decided to give everyone in our department an aptitude test. This was a disaster. Even though my work was praised by everyone I worked with, she decided to summon me to her office to deliver the good news with the compassion of a Dalek "Alex, I have your test results and I'm afraid you don't have the intellectual capacity to continue in this job." These words were devastating, the experimental method of teaching I received until I was seven was still having its effect at the age of twenty-two. I remember the feeling of panic as I explained to her that I had a family to care for and depended on the job, but her insults got worse. "According to the results you have the IQ of someone with Down syndrome, I just can't have you working in my department, you are a liability." I was so shocked that I started speaking in a ridiculous cockney accent as if I had been taken over by the spirit of 'Tiny Tim' in the Charles Dickens story of 'A Christmas Carol'. To be honest, if I was telling someone who possesses a strong Geordie accent that they were being dismissed and this resulted in them becoming a Cockney I would become a little scared, but it was as if she didn't even notice my pathological reaction. Looking back I find it astonishing that I didn't make a complaint against her, but I just accepted her assessment and begged for guidance on how to improve. I remember her answer to my pathetic please for leniency were greeted with an emotionless "You can't get any better than this, you are a liability" Fortunately my other work colleagues were 'down to earth types' and many of them were university educated and used the 'credibility' this brings to change her mind. I managed to keep my job with P & G for the next three years by the skin of my teeth.

I eventually started work with Northumberland County Council who has supported me in personal development which gave me the confidence to advance in my education.

It all sounds pretty negative, as if I am saying "poor me" but if you are going to read my essays I need you to be aware that there are going to be the odd mistakes in spelling and grammar.

As you can imagine publishing any kind of book was going to be a risk but with the help of MS Word and a few emails from friends who wrote in a panic to tell me that I had spelt Coal Miner as Coal Minor I appear to have created a collection of essays that are pretty damn cool and I think you will like them.

Becoming a counsellor involves changing your perspective regarding the self-concept and how other people are perceived. For many in the classroom this can be a very emotional experience which brings into awareness how neurotic we as humans tend to be. Being negative and focusing the mind on events that cause distress is useful in the sense that we are constantly attempting to find a solution to the problem. In the wild you will find that animals are timid because they have evolved a negative thinking process which makes them paranoid and vigilant, ready to escape a predator at any moment. Animals also must fight to maintain dominance in a group so that they can get the best of the food and also become the patriarch who gets to impregnate the females. Humans are no different from the wild animals. We have no biological use for staying positive and seeing the best in people. This is because such a perspective would result in vulnerability and the risk becoming exploited victims of other people's desire for dominance. Seeing the good in those who would potentially take our money, job position, damage our reputation; or even physically harm us, is not useful to our survival. We have evolved to be negative to protect ourselves. Protection from other humans is important. Campaigns against bullying in schools and work tell us quite clearly that humans are still animals and will behave in antisocial ways for all of the above reasons. Criminals commit the most hideous of crimes and although there are differing opinions as to the proportion, it is believed that there is as many as one psychopath in every one hundred people. A psychopath exists without empathy, conscience or compassion and is excellent at taking advantage of the weak and becoming dominant in a group. You can find them in prisons, but the clever ones can be found in management positions, reaching the top of the hierarchy of needs on the bodies of their victims (figuratively speaking). As a counsellor it is important to understand and be aware of the negative side of human nature.

Counsellors are the modern day equivalent of clergy and witchdoctors. People view them as having secret knowledge and hold them in reverence like a guru who is worthy of a following. This is because they are trained to have a therapeutic perspective regarding humans and also develop an understanding of human nature which appears almost psychic to clients. The counsellor who follows a Rogerian perspective views the client as essentially 'Good'. Anyone who has been accepted by their parents, grandparents or other family member as 'good' will know how nurturing and therapeutic it is to be in such an environment. In such an environment an individual does not feel self conscious or unsafe because there is a feeling of acceptance and love. When the therapist offers the same nurturing acceptance to the client then this leads to a greater chance of self acceptance and psychological health in the client. Of course something that is therapeutic may not necessarily represent reality.

Many trainees find their personal therapy and training to be euphoric because they come to an understanding of their own neurosis. Trainee counsellors often report having 'ah ha' moments where their personal understanding becomes clearer and they begin to progress toward psychological efficiency and wellbeing. For many it is comparable, and even accepted as a spiritual experience.

Most counsellors and psychotherapists started as neurotics who claim that through their studies that they found enlightenment and the freedom to "be," with the ability to perceive the potential in people and draw out the best in them. I am happy to say that I am among the neurotics who chose the path of counselling. My enlightenment was not as euphoric as some have experienced it; in fact it made me a little more cynical as I realised that the therapeutic perspective that everyone is 'essentially good' is not accurate.

Cynicism sounds a little anti counselling, as we know it is therapeutic to accept people as 'essentially good,' but I have worked with both the victims and criminals and my perspective on human nature has been affected by both. Being a little cynical is great because it reduces the chances of being disappointed, it also avoids the pangs of guilt that many therapists have when the positive philosophy of sitting happily in the values of an introjected therapist 'ego ideal' is rocked by the experience of, 'stark in your face empirical truth,' which blatantly tells us that actually some people are not 'good.' Accepting a person unconditionally also means accepting them if they do not possess a conscience or empathy, it is something that must be done when working with some criminals. There's no doubt that anyone will thrive and grow in an environment where they are accepted unconditionally. Awareness of this or having just a touch of cynicism is quite useful in working with people who may not fit the theory. I mention this because the following essays where written from a very Rogerion perspective.

The humanistic approach will play a major role in the following essays. The main aim of these essays is to simplify understanding of the processes of human existence without needing to read reams and reams of irrelevant data.

These are genuine student essays that I have adapted for presentations and should not be used as a model for essay writing, but rather they should be read for your enjoyment of the subject. I would love to get your feedback and any recommendations you may have for improvement. Alex@plesseycastle.com

Gestalt Psychotherapy
A holistic View of the Elemental

By Alex H Parker

The human organism has a constant drive toward equilibrium both physically and psychologically this process is called homeostasis. Jean Piaget applied Homeostasis as a drive to achieve cognitive-equilibrium, which assists in developing schemas that are consonant. These schemas are the framework for self-concept and a concept of the environment including the skills required to interact with it. Immanuel Kant states in Critique of Pure Reason.

"At the priori basis of all perception lies pure intuition. (And with regard to pure intuition as representation, time, the form of inner intuition, serve as basis) ; at the priori basis of association lies the pure synthesis of imagination and at the basis of empirical conciseness lies pure apperception, that is to say the pervasive identity of oneself in all representations."

Kant describes here an empirical result in the formation of schemas that are developed through continued experience and association with general deductive principles and previous experience. These phenomena correlate and go through a process called apperception resulting in new schemas and equilibrium. Through the process of apperception a self-concept is formed. Fritz Perls explains this in his book Gestalt therapy page 235

The self is precisely the integrator; it is the synthetic unity, as Kant said. It is the artist of life. It is only a small factor in the total organism/environment interaction, but it plays the crucial role of finding and making the meaning that we grow by.

Gestalt is a German word that means pattern or whole. It started as a cognitive school of psychology that concentrated on visual perception. It demonstrated that people have the drive to find meaning in what they experience and will fill holes (missing information) to complete a gestalt to fulfil this drive for meaning. For example when looking at a random spread of tealeaves in a cup one person may see a dog while another person sees a naked aborigine. Neither person is wrong in what they see because in reality it's just an ambiguous spread of tealeaves but they perceive different things because they apply meaning based upon previous Schema. The complete pattern that is perceived in the tealeaves is called a Gestalt the automatic process of joining gaps between leaves to form the pattern is called the principle of closure. This process is often summarised, as 'the whole is greater than the sum of its parts.' Finding Meaning in our own lives requires forming a gestalt of self based upon empirical experiences of the environment. The boundary between 'Self' and environment is where the interaction can take place through contact this is called the contact boundary. It is here where assimilation of physical resources (food) and psychological resources in the form of values and beliefs takes place-allowing apperception. As a result of this process a self-concept and valuing system is developed which defines future assimilations. This valuing system can either impede or facilitate a person's ability to function. Fritz Perls states on page V (authors note) of Gestalt therapy:

Maturation is a continuous process of transcending environmental support and developing self-support, which means an increasing reduction of dependencies.

This effect can be seen in men who are very authoritarian in their approach to a woman's role. They may assimilate the belief during childhood that women should do all the household chores. When his wife runs off with the milkman leaving him without the basic skills to care for himself, gaps in his development are brought into awareness motivating him to either manipulatively buy his wife a bunch of flowers to avoid the frustration, or grow as a person. Fritz Perls continues to postulate that: if a child is spoilt and deprived of the opportunity to "do for himself," he will develop his own individual brand of psychopathology. He will start to manipulate the environment…to ensure that those intolerable frustrations will not occur again.

Frustration drives the individual constantly toward the achievement of equilibrium by making a gestalt dominate thinking which motivates the individual to go through a process called the Cycle of awareness. In order to achieve equilibrium the individual must be aware of the frustration that mobilises contact and assimilation. Successive failures to complete cycles of awareness and the inhibiting of personal development causes an over dependence on the environment i.e. other people, and consequently leads to growth Stagnation. To illustrate a lorry has two or three wheels on each axle to take the weight of its load. If one tyre bursts the driver can still drive the lorry although it becomes more difficult because he has reduced resources. As more tyres burst the driving of the lorry becomes increasingly difficult until the lorry collapses under its own weight and fails to reach its destination. People can live quite happily with only a few minor cycles unfulfilled, but if their resources are too depleted they may find that they are unable to achieve equilibrium resulting in unfinished business (a gestalt that keeps returning to awareness causing anxiety). Like homeostasis, actualising Tendency constantly drives the individual to equilibrium but is unable to accomplish this if growth stagnation exists. Self-actualisation and self-concept are central to the humanistic model and the functioning of both can be understood by phenomenological introspection. This brings into awareness the subjective experiences of an individual including all manifestations of the psyche physically emotionally and cognitively. Since all aspects of self can be potentially experienced through phenomenology making a complete gestalt of self, possible. Inaccurate self-concept in relation to the environment is caused by a disturbance to the contact boundary, which expresses itself in various forms of defence mechanism that are recognised by a counsellor and used to assist awareness. For example I was asked to counsel a client in a class setting called Elizabeth.

(I will use Elizabeth's example to facilitate an explanation of contact boundaries without meaning to implying any concrete diagnosis. She asked for a pseudonym to be used to protect her confidentiality)

She described dreaming of becoming a dancer when young but became a housewife with several children instead. She has introjected the belief from her mother that dancing is the work of harlots. It could be suggested that Elizabeth had assimilated beliefs without examining them first resulting in introjected ideals. Projection is a way of attributing responsibility that originates from self to the environment. In the case of, Elizabeth who has introjected strong authoritarian values about women dancers, the anger that she feels appears to be projected onto Brittany Spears when watching MTV. She expressed her feelings kinaesthetically as well as verbally.

Elizabeth: That Bloody Britany Spears, teaching people to flaunt them self. Lascivious whore! (Hits her knee).

This projection would give her the perception that it was Britany Spears who is responsible for the way her introjected values and beliefs have made her feel. By attributing blame to Britany Spears as the reason for her feelings Elizabeth accepted no responsibility and thus was powerless to change the way she felt. When Elizabeth hit her knee this may have been an example of Retroflection. This happens when an individual wants to do something to the environment but they express that action toward self instead. For example, when Elizabeth watched Brittany Spears dancing she couldn't go and punch her on the nose, so he expressed her anger by hitting her knee with her fist. Retroflection may also be expressed, as something desired from the environment that is unobtainable. In such cases people may hug themselves when in need of comfort, especially after punching themselves in the knee in anger. Confluence manifests itself if a person has a weak perceptive boundary between ego and environment. What Elizabeth says next may be an example of this.

Elizabeth: If my mam is happy then I'm happy. I don't think I would know what to do without her. I really respect her. I noticed Carla (Elizabeth's daughter) dancing in her bedroom last week when mam was due to arrive. I absolutely freaked.

Elizabeth expressed that she views her mother as an integral part of her life and basis all her actions upon the approval of her family apparently without the interjection of her own Organismic valuing. Her self-concept has become an ambiguous picture where figure (Elizabeth herself) and ground (her family) are indistinguishable rendering her only able to Actualise a family ideal. Confluence is an example of deindividuation. Erich Fromm describes its nature on page 20 of The Fear of Freedom:

They are the ties that connect a child with its mother, the member of a primitive community with its clan and nature, or the medieval man with the Church and his social caste.

According to the principles of Maslow's hierarchy of needs dependence upon the environment for personal growth ends at the social stage. If an individual's self-regard is based upon other people's ideals then the need for esteem will become dependent upon living up to those conditions. It is this that determines whether we self-actualise or actualise an ideal. Acceptance of self is essential for a person to Self-Actualise. Total unconditional acceptance of self leads to the absence of disruptions to the contact boundary and Congruence. Carl Rogers asserted that when faced with aspects of self that don't fit our self-concept then the self-concept is no longer complete as a gestalt. When this happens the individual is in crisis because equilibrium is disrupted causing anxiety until it is restored. Carl Rogers explains this point in the Carl Rogers Reader page 247:

The essential nature of the threat is that if the experience were accurately symbolised in awareness, the self-concept would no longer be a consistent Gestalt, the conditions of worth would be violated, and the need for self-regard would be frustrated. A state of anxiety would exist.

Confluence causes an individual's Ego-boundary to encompass people in the environment and their ideals. The result can be a rejection of aspects of self, which are in opposition to those ideals. An individual may develop defence mechanisms such as those described above to keep the incongruence out of awareness and avoid anxiety. In relation to these defence mechanisms Rogers continues:

This process consists of selective perception or distortion of the experience and/or the denial into awareness of the experience or some portion thereof, thus keeping the total perception of the experience consistent with the individuals self-structure, and consistent with his conditions of worth.

Completing an accurate figure of personality and awareness of unfinished business that his the aim of therapy. It is by combining the two that a correlation can be seen between external events and Personal responsibility. It is the role of the counsellor to bring some of the defence mechanisms such as projection, retroflection, confluence and introjections into awareness so that the client can develop a more accurate perception of their responsibility regarding interactions with the environment and function more effectively with a more accurate perception of self, differentiated from the environment. .

Gestalt Approach skills

Developing an accurate perception of self requires an awareness of orgasmic phenomenology, which is focused on by use of several strategies and techniques. Fritz Perls on page 17 of gestalt therapy states:

The basic endeavour is to assist you to become aware of how you are functioning as an organism and as a person. Since you are the only one who can make the necessary observations, we shall... be dealing with "private events."

This is achieved in by empathic observations of the counsellor. This would include reflecting back kinaesthetic messages that the client may unconsciously communicate through physical movement, posture, breathing, eye movements etc.

Alex: Elizabeth, you just hit yourself in the knee when talking about Brittany Spears dancing. Where did that come from?

Elizabeth: Well, I think I'm annoyed.

Alex: You think you're annoyed?

Elizabeth: Yes, I'm bloody annoyed!

Through my observation Elizabeth was assisted to perceive her defence and have a more complete figure of self from which she could apply meaning. Phenomenology requires complete awareness of what is happening in the present. Although the past may be involved, it is its effect on the present that is of concern and is focused upon. This can often highlight unfinished business; the effect of an incomplete cycle of awareness. Skill is required to overcome the powerful defence mechanisms that can be manifest as awareness is resisted.

Freud stated in the Freud reader page 569:

If what was in question was the operation of an external stimulus, the appropriate method would be flight: with an instinct, flight is of no avail for the ego cannot escape its self. At some later period rejection based on judgement (condemnation) will be found to be a good method to adopt against an instinctual impulse.

Rejection of aspects of self, including painful experiences based on judgement is primarily caused by introjected conditions of worth from the environment that is contrary to our organismic valuing. The rejected aspects of self cannot be escaped from because they are part of our organism. They manifest themselves during therapy by attempts by the client to hide these aspects, rather like the same way a person attempts to hide a love bite on their neck by conspicuously and repetitively pulling their collar over it. Similarly a client may try to avoid aspects of self by behaviour that actually draws attention it by changing the subject and kinaesthetic expressions such as lowering gaze etc.

Alex: I notice when you express anger verbally toward Britany Spears that you smile at the same time.

Elizabeth: Yeh, well, you feel stupid saying I'm angry, feels wrong, like it doesn't suit you; kind of thing.

Alex: Who feels stupid, doesn't suit who?

Elizabeth: (laughs) me. I mean I feel stupid.

The counsellor typically brings the defensive behaviour to the awareness using immediacy so that further examination and assistance can be given to the client to integrate and take responsibility for these parts of self. Unlike person centred therapy, gestalt does not wait until a client makes a decision to explore those aspects in their own time.

Experiments

I had worked with Elizabeth over several weeks and had noticed that the same subject matter was being discussed repetitively although I was convinced that in every session that important insight had occurred. Experiments are used in Gestalt therapy to assist a client to develop their perception of reality through various techniques. For example the empty chair has been used to assist a person to have dialogues with other people or aspects of self that could be featured in dreams and enact the part of each character. This experiment is used widely in Transactional analysis as a way of understanding how an individual's ego states interact.

Insight is also found in dream work where all elements of the dream are approached as a viewpoint of self and enacted by the client.

Lyn Webster explains in the book Dream-work page 42:

It is based on the principle that all the elements of a dream are parts of the dreamer, split off from his ego and struggling to come onto relation with each other. In order to integrate all these parts the dreamer "must become" each one in turn and experience the dream from his, her point of view. Once the different identities are established they can talk or fight with each other (or communicate in other someway) until a resolution is achieved.

I am sceptical about the validity of this theory of dreams but it could still be therapeutic but for different reasons. I believe that parts of the dream that are remembered are the parts that have meaning to the dreamer so they stand out as a Gestalt and are relevant to current apperception and schematic assimilation. However Jung also saw the value of dreams in the process of integrating fragments of self in the form of shadow and archetypes. He called this operation individuation (the opposite of confluence) and made it the focus of analytical psychology. I felt that Elizabeth could benefit from seeing her life as a whole rather than the fragmented set of different patterns without any connection. I had hoped that frequent summaries would assist her to do this but I was starting to become frustrated and felt that it was time to use immediacy to express my concerns.

Alex: Elizabeth, I've noticed over the past few weeks that we've had sessions that are virtually the same, almost a repeat of the week before. How do you feel about what I've just said?

Elizabeth: I know. I'm just worried that my daughter will take on this stupid dancing. It would kill my mum if she did.

Alex: Okay, how would you feel about explaining your life to me by using playing cards?

I explained that they were normal playing cards that she could pick different ones from the pack that feel right to represent parts of her life and explain those parts of her life as she did so, placing them on a table between us.

Alex: I noticed when you put the card for your mum on the table it was on top of the card representing yourself, whereas the card for Carla is further away next to the card for your dad.

Elizabeth thinks for a few minutes. And I interject.

Alex: What's going through your mind Elizabeth?

Elizabeth: Dad and Carla are quite close. (Deep sigh).

Alex: That's a very deep sigh Liz. What are you feeling?

Elizabeth: (hands move to cover face) God, deep….deep sadness.

This appeared to help her to recognise connections in her experiences by looking at her life as a gestalt on the table in front of her and began to experience emotions that had existed before, but not in awareness. This catharsis assisted her to have a clearer self-concept in relation to the environment, as she became more phenomenologicaly aware. These new schema could be assimilated through the process of apperception until equilibrium exists. She described the experience after the session as very insightful.

I have found that when gestalt theory is compared to the other major approaches to therapy that there appears to be a coherent theme in all theoretical assumptions and psychological perspectives. Studying this subject has assisted me to appreciate the complexities and frailty of the human psyche and also its ability to heal when environmental conditions are favourable.   ☐ Alex H Parker. (2005)

Loss and Grief

By Alex H Parker

"The beginning of being released from suffering is to investigate one of the primary causes: resistance to change."

(Dalai Lama. Cutler. 1998) p163.

Humans approach change on an individual level, which it is difficult to standardise. It can bring happiness as a person finds they have won the lottery, have new breast implants or the acquisition of a new girlfriend that looks like Christina Aguilera. It can also bring suffering when cherished attachments are severed such as the loss of a job, development of a disability or the death of a loved one.

The primary cause of resistance to change is often related to our attachment to environmental resources. All attachments represent a resource that can contribute toward self-concept and the ability to predict and interact with the environment. Many of the resources are represented in the social stage of 'The hierarchy of needs' which is where the primary need for positive regard is required from others so that self-esteem can develop. The quality of positive regard or acceptance experienced from friends and family is used to asses our own value and from this we develop a level of self-regard which renders us either secure in our sense of self-worth or to develop anxious attachments to people who provide positive regard or love. We may express this by conforming behaviour to those people's ideals. This is a humanistic perspective of a psychodynamic process. Freud explains in Mourning and melancholia (1989). p584:

"The patient represents his ego to us as worthless, incapable of any achievement and morally despicable; he reproaches himself, vilifies himself and expects to be cast out and punished."

A child develops either 'conditional' or 'unconditional positive self-regard' based on their social environment with family and friends. This becomes the base of the child's developing ego and self-concept. The ego's role is to protect and provide regulated pleasure to the id. This process contributes to the development of superego which develops as values and beliefs are assimilated as introjects. These introjects control behaviour with a view to maintaining the acquisition of positive regard from the environment and also maintain self-esteem this process is typified in the Oedipus complex.

If superego devalues the process of ego and organismic valuing, then the loss of an attachment figure will be complicated and the individual will find difficulty in adapting to the loss if that attachment figure was a source for acquiring conditional positive self-regard. If someone relies on the social environment as their main source of positive regard then actualising an ideal based on an external locus of evaluation will lose its meaning making the maintenance of current self-concept valueless when the attachment figure is no longer available to provide positive regard. The provision of positive regard may become an increased necessity as feelings of ambivalence toward the deceased can be a source of further turmoil as the individual deals with negative feelings toward an individual that they have assimilated into superego and rely upon for positive regard while at the same time feeling negative to the very same internalised aspect of self that cannot be appeased by a weak ego. The reality of the death may be kept from awareness as an ego defence until disruption to continuity can be experienced and accommodated.

The effect of the Superego may be evident in the Peter Marris theory, which suggests that Humans have an innate tendency to maintain continuity and resist change; he called this the conservative impulse. According to Marris, the Conservative impulse assists a person to predict their environment and feel secure. The conservative impulse resists change but with continued exposure with reality the change is accommodated. Marris put forward that the conservative impulse, minimises disruption to the established construct so that a structure of meaning can still be applied to experience. In this way Marris postulates a process of change that is adaptable by integrating an individual's perceived reality with experience. Resistance between the conservative impulse, which provided security and the adapted structure of meaning, which is more representative of reality to which the conservative impulse can integrate, can be represented by the struggle between ego and superego. I believe that the conservative impulse is not an innate part of the human psyche but rather an indicator of the severity of a weak ego. Freud agrees that exposure to reality can assist with the process of change but this depends on the internal relationship between ego and superego. The executive superego complicates grief as it suppresses ego so no accommodation can be made for change. The conservative impulse and super ego may be significant factors in a process that Freud called reinvestment. The conservative impulse requires familiar surroundings in order to aid prediction and avoid anxiety; it will therefore use the template of an executive superego to reinvest the energy of one relationship to a similar one. This is often seen in the process of transference where a man will marry a woman who is similar to his previous wife or when experiencing the transition to adulthood marries a woman who reminds him of his mother. However in the absence of an adequate transference figure libidinal reinvestment can be any form of substitution including hobbies and career. It could be argued that this libidinal reinvestment is always a sign of a weak ego as the non-social reinvestment maybe based on internalised values of the attachment figure; however I have found no research to support this. A strong ego is able to facilitate grief by recognising the reality of the loss and gradually creating a new construct of existence and available resources. Parks asserts that Psychic equilibrium is restored when the transition from the assumed reality with the attachment figure is successively concluded by the accommodation of reality without the attachment figure.

Parks (1972) explains:

"Psychosocial transitions are the times when we reassess our picture of the world and our means of being part of it. They are experienced as imprinting upon us, but their effects include major changes in the heartland of the self... we need protection, reassurance, time to recoup, and help in developing-blue prints for the future."

Parks acknowledges that the change experienced in grief represents not only a change in the environment but also a requirement to change personally. Through his model of grief Parks represents the conclusion of change as the gaining of a new identity and adoption of new social roles. This would involve a gradual process rather than an immediate acceptance as ego assimilates the change gradually to minimise pain to the id. This is further explained by Melanie Kleine (1952) who identified the psyche's tendency to assess individuals as either good or bad based on their role in fulfilling the desires of the id. In short Klein asserts that attachment figures either fulfil the desires for the id or not and become bad persecutory objects or good objects based on their momentary provision of gratification. Since both negative and positive feelings are attributed to the same attachment figure, ambivalence exists leading to feelings of guilt. This is because feelings of resentment as well as love are experienced toward the good attachment figure when they die. This is because they have withdrawn their provision of positive regard by being absent. This abandonment is a bad persecutory role by the attachment figure, as they are permanently unable to gratify the id. In many experiences of grief the abandonment through death could be correlated to the threat of abandonment that is feared by children when they feel insecure. An adult who has never outgrown the need of positive regard from their attachment figure may react to this as if they have been punished. This fear of punishment or persecution by the dead could explain why some African tribes go through exhaustive rituals and superstitions to appease the dead as part of their everyday culture and also more generally explain the origin of belief in an afterlife and religion. I feel it is important to keep the spiritual aspect of human grief experience in mind as through its rituals it often contributes the psychological accommodation of loss through funerals, and the creation of an existential schema of death that defines how painful the experience of grief is.

John Bowlby (1969/73) suggests that all psychiatric disorders can be traced back to the quality of affectional bonding in infancy. According to Bowlby any experience of temporarily losing an attachment figure through day care etc at a time in the infant's life when they are unable to understand why their attachment figure has gone will contribute to insecure attachment or fear of abandonment that persists into adult life.

This can be witnessed in individuals who are overly clingy and possessive to a relationship where anxiety in unwarranted and also contribute to complicated grief.

As I have written the above I feel quite irritated that most research concentrates on variations of a psychodynamic perspective. It all sounds very intelligent and I'm sure it's a starting point for attempting to understand grief and loss but it completely fails to address the compete holistic experience of human beings and reduces the process of change to varying degrees of neurosis based on ego strength and past experience. It also risks classifying all humans as functioning in the same uniformed way. For example, these theories completely fail to address the existential issues that are involved in loss and their effect on the religious and philosophical rituals practised during the grief process. This is mainly because all these theorists are white European Jews or Christians. Existential issues are again generally ignored when theorists have devised stages of grief based again on a dogmatic Eurocentric viewpoint.

It is discouraging to see theorists struggling to provide a rigid dogmatic 'one theory fits all' model of grief, and even more discouraging to see counsellors rigidly following them as if they were holy doctrine depending on their current popularity based on book sales.

Elizabeth Kubler-Ross (2005) is often quoted as having the classic model. She notes that in her experience that grief for the dying and for the bereaved involves a process of Denial, anger, bargaining, depression and acceptance. She states:

"They are tools to help us frame and identify what we may be feeling… Not everyone goes through all of them in a prescribed order."

Although Kubler-Ross acknowledges that this model is just to help to identify feelings that *May* be present, I feel she completely distracts from the idiosyncratic experiences of the individual, reducing the effectiveness of counsellors, care workers and all who view it as scientifically verified. In my opinion this risks removing the ability of empathy by approaching clients with a very narrow frame of reference. Although these attributes of grief can be manifest in some people, I have been presented with no evidence in her books that they are all a necessary part of grief apart from case studies with clients who are dying which is generalised to fit all grief, which appears to satisfy the author's bias experience with the dying. I might change my mind about this model through experience but I don't intend to approach my practice with this as my schema of grief. In contrast to Kubler-Ross's passive observation model, Warden (1983) writes an intelligent and practical approach for counsellors to use when facilitating uncomplicated grief. It involves ten principles that generally speaking assist in helping the client to actualise the loss, express and become aware of their holistic experience of grief, which culminates in emotional relocation of the deceased, which is similar in principle to Freud's reinvestment theory. He also suggests four tasks involved in grief, which broadly speaking involves accommodation of new circumstances before psychological relocation of deceased. I feel warden's approach has more practical use for he counsellor than Kubler-Ross, because it can be applied in a therapeutic context rather than just a process to be observed by a counsellor with a 'Knowing' look on their face. I also think Wardens approach is general enough to accommodate cultural and existential individuality, although it is a common thread in both approaches that acceptance of the reality of loss is important to the process of successful grieving. Stroebe also provided a model of grief that addresses the incidental life occurrences that exist as an individual moves between the experience and emotional difficulty of grief, which is loss orientated and restoration orientated experiences that keep the emotional distress out of awareness or to a degree, which is manageable so that the individual can function. As the life experiences keep the loss to a manageable degree then the process of actuation of loss and acceptance can run its course. This model appears to acknowledge that while the process of grief is significant it is not the only thing that happens in life while waiting for its conclusion and also acknowledges the unpredictable contribution of every day experience which effects its successful conclusion. I personally feel that awareness of these models and theories is useful to know as a very rough and general guide but are restricted by their lack of accommodation of human diversity.

I approach all change including grief and general human development as a constant drive for equilibrium so that actualising tendency can guide the individual to self-healing through accommodation of the changing environment. I view all change in the same way and feel that Paige's model of human development can also be applied to all aspects of human development and change. I say this because it focuses on experience that leads to learning and development, which is evident in the successful conclusion of grief. These are disequilibrium, accommodation, and assimilation culminating in equilibrium. Although this is a cognitive model I feel that it can be applied holistically without the assumptions implied by psychodynamic perspective. I also think that a cognitive model better explains the generally agreed theme from all researchers for successful grief, which is actuating of the loss and relocation of the deceased. The cognitive perspective is necessary in my opinion as it is the constructs of reality and the individuals place in that reality that require accommodation. However I feel that although a cognitive perspective addresses the source of complicated grief its affect is holistic and therefore must be dealt with by using a humanistic approach.

© Alex H Parker 2006

On Becoming Neurotic
Transactional Analysis
& Humanistic Approach.

Congruence or genuineness is a term that Carl Rogers said was essential for all counsellors to have in order to be competent. Congruence along with empathy and unconditional positive regard is what make up the three core qualities of person centred approach to counselling. Congruence is the most important part of the three qualities because it involves being self-aware which Rogers believed was essential for the counsellor to be if he was to embark on getting to know and understand clients. This would lead to empathy and unconditional positive regard. Jan Sutton and William Stewart stated in their book learning to counsel:

"Genuiness (congruence) is the precondition for empathy and unconditional positive regard. Effective counselling depends wholly on the degree to which the counsellor is integrated and genuine."

According to Rogers Congruence means avoiding putting on a façade being aware of how we feel and allowing this to be expressed verbally and non-verbally. A façade is often used in every day encounters as a form of politeness. When someone asks how we are in a brief meeting it would be unusual to go into detail about our haemorrhoids that are giving us jip because the situation would be inappropriate, so the normal response is "I'm fine." This would be not a response that would lead to neurosis but if a person was to go to the doctors and tell them that they were in pain because they had a head ache and not haemorrhoids then this would be a façade, cover up, and incongruent. Incongruence can hide the truth from others and it also hides the truth from our self. For example a sixteen year old boy called Walter, wants to go to college and learn ballet and eventually do swan lake to an audience in a big well known theatre in London, one day Walter and his father are watching television together and swan lake comes on. The father then starts to call the men doing ballet homosexuals, he then opens his paper and says "son you'll be a coal miner like your father, a real man." Walter gives up his ambition to learn ballet and becomes a coal miner, deeply unhappy with his career. Walter, in this instance was not congruent he decided to live his life in a way that others decided it should be lead and ignored his drive to develop his own interests which is his ability to self-actualise. Walter also learned from this that he only received love from his father if he obeyed his father's conditions of worth or approval. This is called conditional positive regarded because

Walters father only gives him approval (positive regard) if Walter lives buy his father's values, (conditions). Speaking of unconditional positive regard, Rogers States in The Carl Rogers Reader:

'It means that there are no conditions of acceptance, no feeling of "I only like you if you are thus and so," it means a "prizing" of the person'.

The need for unconditional positive regard must be fulfilled if a person is to be become congruent. Becoming congruent means to accept self and have unconditional positive self-regard. Rogers states:

"A need for positive self-regard develops as a learned need developing out of the association of self-experience with the satisfaction or frustration of the need for positive regard."

Experience of positive regard from others is how we develop a concept of ourselves and our value in whatever roles we play. If our positive self- regard is based on the conditions and values of other people, then we will not be acceptant of self. If our actualising tendency encourages us to deviate from those external values this will render an individual incongruent and unable to self-actualise.

Life Positions

Some people who have only received positive regard during their lives may view themselves as OK and others as OK in other words positive regard to others and self.

In Transactional Analysis developed by Dr. Eric Berne there are four life positions which a person will display in their interactions toward others and self, these are:

I'm Ok - You're Ok.

I'm Ok - You're not Ok

I'm not Ok - You're Ok

I'm not Ok - You're not Ok

These for life positions are developed at the same time that we develop a concept of ourselves and others, and is thought that all persons adopt one of these life positions as how they view and value others and self for the rest of their lives, or until they have received counselling.

Like positive self-regard, each life position is developed as a result of interactions with others and how these others valued us and interacted with us as a child.

First position: I'm OK – Your OK

This is a mentally healthy position. This type of person can solve problems constructively their expectations are likely to be valid; they will accept the value and significance of others.

This life position is ideal and will result from constant positive regard; congruence and self-actualising will be present.

Second position I'm ok – You're not Ok

This person will feel victimised or persecuted, and so victimises and persecutes others. They blame others for their miseries and may adopt paranoid behaviour that can lead to homicide. This person would need to work through their difficulties and accept responsibility for their own decisions and actions. Not accepting responsibility is in opposition to actualising tendency and results in incongruence.

Third position I'm not Ok – You're Ok

Person may feel powerless when they compare themselves to others. Can cause them to withdraw, experience depression, and in severe cases become suicidal.

This person is incongruent as their view of themselves is based on the values of others and prevents them from self-actualising.

Fourth position I'm not Ok – You're not Ok

Those who lose interest in living who in extreme cases commit suicide or homicide or both. This would be characteristic of a severely mentally ill person. This person would probably need some sort of psychiatric treatment and would be working in opposition to actualising tendency, the result would be incongruence.

Walter accepted his father's wishes that he follow in his footsteps so that he could continue to receive positive regard from his father, even if this was conditional. From doing things according to his father's wishes he could achieve what is called in Transactional Analysis as positive strokes.

Strokes are any act implying recognition of another's presence; they can be given in the form of an actual physical touch or by some form of acknowledgement such as a look, a word or a gesture. All people have a hunger or a need for either positive or negative strokes and this will often determine what they do with their time. Positive strokes assist a person to develop emotionally healthy, and maintain self-esteem. A parent who picks up their child and tells them they love them, express positive strokes. They are genuine expressions of affection or appreciation or compliments. Positive strokes help an individual feel valued and are given by expressing positive regard which will lead to positive self-regard. Negative strokes are expressions of devaluing a person, discounting their significance; it may be expressed in the same way as positive strokes but with negative messages to the recipient through sarcasm, false compliments violence and verbal abuse. Walter has received positive strokes during his life from his father as long as he conforms to his father's beliefs and values, if he in any way deviates he could be at risk of receiving negative strokes from his father. So to continue to feel valued and receive conditional positive regard he conforms to his father's beliefs attitudes and values, he may even adopt some of his prejudices.

Carl Rogers states:

"The majority of values are introjected from other individuals or groups, but are regarded by him as his own. The source or locus of evaluation on lost matters lies outside himself. The criterion by which his values are set is the degree that will cause him to be loved and accepted."

Ego states.

Walter still obeys the values and beliefs of his dead father when he no longer is able to receive positive regard from him is partially explained by the nature of Ego states. Now Walters son has expressed a desire to be a nurse and plans to go to college, Walter responds that 'male nurses are effeminate and that they may well be homosexuals and that he should work down the mine like a real man.' Walter says this aware that he is not happy with his career but expresses that he believes that it is the best course of action for his son. When Walter expressed himself in this instance he was expressing not his own values but that of his father or Parent as if running a tape recording. The recorded set of values known in Transactional Analysis as the Parent ego within him was not only making Walter deeply unhappy and incongruent, but ran the risk of making his son incongruent too, reducing his freedom to self-actualise.

At work Walter, finds it incredibly difficult to relate to the other male colleagues. He feels foolish all the time and has difficulty communicating on their level. He feels that if doesn't have their approval and that he is not a valued member of the team. Many of his work colleagues are similar to his father in many ways in their attitudes and values, and when he speaks with them he feels like a Child longing for positive strokes.

The Child Ego state has the emotional reactions recorded from our early life. These reactions are not rational or thought out, they are automatic, and demonstrate emotional memories to a specific stimulus. In the case of his emotional reaction to his work colleagues, it may be triggered by generalised emotional memories of his father (Parent) recalling emotional memories and reactions as present experiences. For example Walter was knocked to the floor by a large dog that wanted to play when he was five years old, the result in his later years is that he has an apparently irrational fear of dogs, and when he sees a dog an emotional response is activated that makes him feel exactly as he did when he was five years old. This emotional reaction will happen even if he can't remember the event. This happens because emotions are stored as memories as well as sight, sound, taste touch and smell, but the emotion is the only part of the memory that comes into consciousness in this instance. He may even develop a generalised emotional response to things that remind him of dogs, such as a fur coat or a picture of a dog. In the case of his emotional reaction to his work colleagues, it may be triggered by generalised emotional memories of his Parent inducing a feeling of not ok. Walter feels most at peace when he's working on machines. He knows how to fix them and he is able to solve problems that the machines have developed. When working in this way he is more like a computer than a man because there is no emotion involved in problem solving. When Walter is problem solving he is being objective and is in his Adult ego state. According to Transactional Analysis Parent, adult and child are present within all humans and these interact internally. For example a young man is offered a cigarette and he is curious of what the experience of smoking is like, the curiosity he experiences comes from the Child ego state. As he is contemplates accepting the offer of a cigarette his internal parent ego says it is wrong and unsociable to smoke, so now he has a dilemma causing incongruence between the two ego states no matter what decision he makes. His adult Ego may solve the dilemma by giving an objective viewpoint, and may decide that one cigarette will not make you addicted or it may decide that it would be unnecessary and unhealthy. In either case the individual has made their decision, rationally and can take personal responsibility for the outcome. This would result in a congruent decision no matter what the decision was. After a person understands how they interact within themselves they can listen to their feelings in certain situations and view them objectively from the adult ego to dispel incongruence.

A student of Eric Berne, Thomas A Harris M.D states in his book I'm Ok You're Ok:

"One of the important functions of the adult is to examine the data in the parent, to see whether or not it is true and still applicable today, and then to accept or reject it: and to examine the child to see whether the feelings there are appropriate to the present or are archaic and in response to archaic data. The goal is not to do away with the adult and child but to be free to examine these bodies of data."

It is through strengthening the Adult ego's influence that people can understand themselves better, and continue or begin to develop as an autonomous person and achieve congruence. The counsellor who uses client centred approach will always give the client an environment where unconditional positive regard is present and will demonstrate this through empathy skills, this will fulfil a basic need for recognition which is a fundamental positive stroke and free the client to express themselves without the need to conform to established values in order to receive positive strokes or positive regard. At an appropriate time in the counselling relationship some of the principles of Transactional Analysis are explained in a group or workshop setting, or progressively during the client counsellor relationship. Transactional Analysis gives the client a new concept of how their Ego states operate, and enables them to express themselves in a non-abstract way; this will assist self-exploration and self-awareness. When the Adult ego is strengthened the result is that the Parent and child no longer make decisions without the examination and influence of the adult ego. Positive self-regard and congruence can be achieved, as the individual will be able to use their strengthened Adult to resolve internal conflicts. It could be argued that if the adult ego were dominant most of the time then an individual would become incongruent because the needs of child and adult are suppressed. Activating adult could also be used as a form of defence against negative emotions which would block effective examination of self and empathy with others; this is why a counsellor would be required to assist the client so as to not leave him to use unsupported self-help knowledge. I have found researching this material useful in understanding myself and my internal interactions and the effect they have on me when I interact with other individuals. I have noticed when interacting with clients at work that I am able to draw out the adult ego in people if I use the adult ego myself, but also that some people have an under developed adult ego and respond to it as parent ego hooking their child ego. I feel in such cases that it is important to be respectful to the child ego in other individuals and approach them in a congruent way, which appears to facilitate communication and strengthen the Adult ego in them so that they can become a ballet dancer if they so wish.

© 2003 Alex H Parker

Relationship Counselling
Alex H Parker

Relationship counselling is one of the most rewarding endeavours a therapist can embark on. To assist two individuals to communicate and arrive to a clear awareness about their situation and each other's perception of their situation creates a venue for permanent improvement in their general situation. The following discussion offers a brief overview of the popular approaches to relationship counselling. In The UK the 'Relate' is best known for delivering relationship counselling. They use a Three Stage model which includes theories that focus on facilitating counselling with couples. This model addresses psychodynamic processes of attachment and social conditioning. The first stage involves creating a therapeutic environment where the core conditions of Person Centred Approach are provided to encourage exploration of the problem and reduces the need for ego defences. When Ego defences are reduced, learning of the past becomes accessible; this in turn assists individual clients to understand perceptions and behaviour of the present. I believe that the Person Centred Core Conditions are the key facilitating factor in creating this environment but psychodynamic perspectives also provide models that address issues that are unconscious and often include taboo subjects that are avoided in some cultural systems with the intention of necessitating collective introjection and maintain social equilibrium. Couple counselling literature doesn't appear to attribute too much credence to Person Centred Approach. It is alluded to briefly on page 42 of 'Counselling Couples in Relationships,' regarding empathy but then appears to discredit its basis by stating that a counsellor only needs to 'suspend judgment' rather than to be non-judgmental. This view is also endorsed on page 20 of the book 'Doing Couple Therapy' (formally "The Crowded Bed"), by Toby Bobes. I believe that if a counsellor becomes aware that an issue has affected them then it is an indicator of a personal issue that has not been addressed, which could inhibit therapy. I believe that to protect impartiality of the counsellor 'Bracketing off' is more appropriate than suspending judgment.

Erving Polster (1973) states:

The distinction is that in bracketing off, one is establishing priorities as to what is most important at that time and not allowing interfering concerns to immobilise him. He does not wipe out the concerns, which seem irrelevant to his temporary engagement, but will return to them later on.

This highlights the need for relationship counsellors to have worked through personal issues and have regular supervision. This will contribute to a therapeutic empathic non-bias environment.

The second stage of the relate approach is where exploration of the past social learning and the uncovering of unconscious process takes place. The theories that are focused on are the Life Stage Model, Object Relations, Triangular Relationships Model, Attachment Model, Systems Theory and the effect of Cultural Perspectives. I feel that Transactional Analysis complements all these theories, except Life Stage Model which addresses specific tasks that must be fulfilled during life stages that if not completed cause anxiety when unresolved conflicts are regressed until successfully negotiated. These theories provide a model to understand the numerous ways that humans learn, interact and develop a self-concept. An individual who comes to counselling seeks psychological equilibrium. This means that incongruities, environmental changes such as loss are readdressed and accommodated. In couple counselling equilibrium is sought within the relationship. The counsellor helps the couple to identify the resources that strengthen homeostasis. Dealing with more than one client in a counselling situation requires not only the nurturing of authenticity in each individual but also the existence of rapport that is enhanced by empathy. This will foster honest communication and the lowering of ego defences as trust develops. In couples counselling it would be taken for granted that Authentic Rapport does not exist in the relationship just as in individual counselling the client is assumed to be incongruent. The counsellor enters into a relationship with couples with the role of communication facilitator. This is initially accomplished by providing the environment where both parties have the space to tell their story and express any problem from their own 'frame of reference' until rapport is established individually with the counsellor, then when trust exists and a working alliance established the process of facilitation can continue, with both parties ideally feeling equally valued by the counsellor and ego-defences reduced. As each member listens to the frame of reference of the partner rapport and empathy between them could eventually strengthen to a point where resolutions can be made independently of the counsellor. This is easier said than done. Each person in the counselling relationship, including the counsellor has a social construct of reality that contributes to perception and automatic responses originating from the unconscious. As the counselling progresses the counsellor may feel automatically angry or frightened regarding one client in the room because they remind the counsellor unconsciously of internal objects such as an abusive Father or may feel protective toward a client who reminds them of their daughter. This will be discussed later when transference and counter-transference is covered but it does reaffirm that suspending judgment is ineffective if it's based on unconscious automatic reactions. For example I remember an interview between Russell Hearty and the singer Grace Jones that I am going to fictionalise a bit. Russell Hearty turned his back to Grace Jones to interview another guest and was immediately punched by the infuriated vocalist for what she perceived to be a rude action. This may have been because he reminded her of her brother who was rude but conformed to etiquette after a beating. It is interesting to note that as he attempted to explain his action from a passive foetal position that he could have been the manifestation of counter transference as he was unconsciously responding as he did with his abusive Mother who he could pacify by curling up in a ball and conforming to her requirements. If Russell Hearty and Grace Jones were a married couple then this would be an interesting case study for relationship counselling.

The couple have come to counselling because Grace is unhappy with Russell's rude obnoxious attitude toward her. Russell did not want to come to counselling and feels embarrassed about his perceived failure as a 'man.' He mentions that Grace spends too much time with her Mother who instigates trouble by gossiping about his failings as a Husband and Father. This relationship between the couple and Graces Mother appears relevant to Triangular Relationship Model. The couples bond appears weakened by the distrust that Russell experiences as a result of feeling persecuted by Grace and her Mother. By entering counselling a new triangular relationship is established where trust is fostered by the counsellor. The first triangular relationship experienced by Russell was the relationship he had with his parents. He always desired the love of his Mother but found that his authoritarian Father received the attention he craved. Bowlby (1969) appears to indicate that social needs of love and belonging have a greater effect on behaviour than the need for physical sustenance, he states:

From empirical observation we suggest that the young child's hunger for his Mother's love and presence is as great as his hunger for food.

In order to attract love of his Mother and acceptance from his Father he modelled himself on his Father. (This is a shortened version of the Oedipus complex). This requires introjection of his Father's values, beliefs and behaviours. Russell became authoritarian in his behaviour toward others and also felt guilty if he failed to live to these introjected ideals. It was as if his Father was still living inside his head scolding him or praising him on his actions. This affected his feelings of self-worth and so in order to maintain self-esteem he would constantly adjust his behaviour to obtain the admiration of his introjected parents and other authoritarian figures such as Grace and her family that he perceived to be similar to them. This is in agreement with Rogers (1989), he States:

In order to receive approval and love, we learn to suppress those feelings and expressions of ourselves that are deemed unacceptable to the important caretakers in our lives.

Adapting behaviour to the ideals of significant others results in personal desires from the ID and the organismic valuing system being silenced by overpowering introjects which are stored in the Superego. When Grace met Russell she fell in love immediately. There was no rational process involved just instantaneous love. This is because her unconscious mind perceived him to be similar to the stored mental object of her Father whom she had internalised as the image of the perfect man. In other words she projected feelings onto Russell that really belonged to her dad because of initially perceived similarities. This is the process of transference. Transference is common but to recognise it requires the ability to examine introjects. A strong Superego suppresses the reality testing hypotheses of a weak Ego. The effect of an overly dominant superego is best explained by Object Relation's theory. Klein (1952) states:

The superego is the internalised representative of the person's most important objects, his parents, the internal residue of his earliest and most intense emotional ties. It is the system of all morality, conscious and unconscious.

Because this process is unconscious the counsellor will facilitate awareness of this process by examining the internalised objects that exists in the mental reputation of family systems of the past and correlate them to the present relationships. A family system like a biological system has its own mechanisms of homeostasis to maintain equilibrium. Equilibrium can be maintained by healthy accommodation of changes to family dynamics through marriage, deaths etc, it can also be superficially maintained by unhealthy ego defences that dogmatically keep the status quo by the collective acceptance of introjects. For example when I started courting my wife I was initially rejected by her family who's catchphrase is 'bloods thicker than water." Eventually I was accepted as part of the system but on reflection it was only after we had children who were perceived as blood relatives and restore equilibrium. Part of the difficulty that Russell and Grace have is the role attribution that they have introjected from both family systems. The Male role is perceived to be that of a traditional gentleman whom has integrity built on the foundation of rules and regulations. The difficulty is that the perception of this role is devoid of ambiguities and therefore Russell is either perfectly successful or a complete failure in this role. Graces Father died when she was young. He was a religious man and authoritarian insisting on traditional etiquette and withheld love from his family if they did not conform to his expectations. If the other siblings in the family including Grace did anything that might upset her Father, her Mother would beat them and justify his actions with a verse from the Bible such as "*Spare the Rod, spoil the child*". Grace internalised this method of dealing with non-conformists. It appears that Russell was initially accepted by Graces family because of his similarity to Graces Dad but is now being rejected because of his failure to be a perfect representation of him. Although Russell is authoritarian he is also atheist while Graces family are strict Christians. When Russell refuses to baptise the children he is perceived to be not fulfilling his adopted role and is ostracised by Graces family for bring immoral. This situation now brings the conflict of a cultural context into play where the accommodation must be made to the collective family perceptions to restore equilibrium. I myself have experienced similar expectations in my family system. Some of my family are part of an authoritarian religious group that do not associate socially with people unaffiliated with the church. I have found myself shunned by them for not continuing religious activities. This rejection protects the group system by introducing the concept of the church members being a spiritual family who maintain the systems equilibrium by withholding affection until the perpetrator conforms to the systems values. This method is effective as any who have been brought up in the church and later leave normally return within a few years. This maybe because the individuals on the outside are part of systems that do not fit the introjections of the church and the only method of receiving human needs of love and acceptance is to return to the church which further reinforces the perception that church introjections are reality. Eric Berne (1972) states:

That is why milk is not enough for baby monkeys and human infants; they also need the sound and smell and warmth and touch of mothering or else they wither away, just like grown ups do if there is no one to say hello to them.

The need for belonging appears to motivate behaviour and will adapt their behaviour to gain what Berne called strokes. Strokes are an act of acknowledgment that is either positive or negative. In childhood Russell would long for positive regard from his parents but found that when his behaviour was acceptable that they ignored him. However when his behaviour was rude this incurred their wrath and he was beaten. He learned that he would only receive acknowledgement from his parents when he was rude. After his beating he became sad and dejected. Much to the disgust of his Father, Russell was then provided with positive strokes in the form of comfort from his guilt ridden Mother who, which had the added bonus of fulfilling the desires of the Oedipus complex. This scenario becomes a psychological game and provides Russell with a strategy of how to gain love and belonging, which ultimately contributes to a life script. The psychological games become part of a family system where social roles and self-concepts are established. A system of games becomes a life script where individuals go through an evaluation process with prospective partners, which is largely unconscious and based on the effect at introjects and transference to assess if they will fit a role for which there is a vacancy in their life script. Claude Steiner (1997) explains:

Though games are failed hurtful attempts to get positive strokes, every completed game gives the player a payoff: it confirms a certain view of the world that the player has chosen to adopt. This enables the game player to see his life as coherent and intelligible, even though his worldview is negative.

When Russell desires affection he becomes rude starting his game with his rebellious child as executive. This hooks Graces critical parent that evaluates behaviour based on introjects of her Father, and then she takes on the characteristics of her Father and beats Russell. Russell's rebellious child becomes an Adapted child rendering him passive, and dejected taking on characteristics similar to Graces brother after he was beaten. Grace reacts to his behaviour and feels compassion and guilt as she projects this internalised object onto Russell, which moves her to take on the characteristics of her internalised Grandma which moves her from Critical parent to Nurturing Parent providing Russell with his goal of acceptance and love as happened with his Mother. The end result of their somewhat provocative and violent game is that they end up very close and affectionate. They have split off any conscious awareness of each other's negative projections and transference being aware of the desired characteristics only. Russell's maladaptive behaviour can also be attributed to insecure attachment. His parents were emotionally absent until he misbehaved which further reinforced his misbehaviour. It is interesting to note that this relationship appears devoid of Adult Ego. This means reality testing is not functioning on a level to where the couple are aware of their responsibility for colluding and creating this problem themselves. The third stage of counselling in the relate approach is the action stage. This stage includes the interventions of the counsellor in the delivery of therapeutic technique. This requires the counsellor to use the information from stage two to bring incongruities into awareness, reframe perceptions and address maladaptive behaviour. Stage three also makes use of visual activities such as stones or other objects that can be used to represent the present or the past relationships and then analyse their findings with the counsellor's observations. Drawing genograms are also useful for clients to do individually and compare to each other, which can further facilitate authentic communication and enhance the ability to see from the other partners 'frame of reference.' Behaviour modification requires the communication of specifics about what each individual would like to change in their partner. This can bring into awareness aspects that have been split off from the partner's self-concept. In short Relates approach is to facilitate communication and empathy between partners by therapeutic environment, the provision of theory to explain relationship process and practical techniques to enhance awareness and strategies. I believe that relationships based on mutual unconditional acceptance of oneself and their partner (or ex-partner) is the foundation of the fully functioning relationship. Unconditional acceptance is the active ingredient in Person Centred approach and can be learned by clients as they become aware their own authentic feelings as well as being empathic regarding their partners frame of reference. A successful conclusion based on truth and understanding will only be facilitated when both sides are equally committed to the process but even if only one individual is committed to a solution then their own progress will assist a beneficial outcome for 50% of those in attendance but will the percentage will increase if we consider the family that will be benefited when these qualities are applied outside the counselling room.

Alex H Parker © 2006

Love, Attachment and Self Concept: Humanistic Perspective

By Alex H Parker

Carl Rogers and Abraham Maslow are the main influences in Humanistic Psychology, which concentrates on subjective thoughts and feelings, self-concept, self-determination and the realisation of potential. Abraham Maslow called it the third force in psychology because it approaches humans as a whole rather than a product of biological mechanisms as is asserted by behaviourist or as a product of unconscious innate drives as asserted by psychoanalysis. It is a person approach to psychology because it focuses on phenomenological experiences of individuals that cannot be quantified in an artificial laboratory environment due to the fact that what is phenomenological cannot be observed because of its subjective nature. Phenomenology is literally the study of internal experiences including thoughts and feelings independent of external stimulus. This makes validation of hypotheses difficult. Field studies can usually be applied in a person approach but they can only focus on behaviour that is observable but unable to attribute to the subjective experience and motivations. The Humanistic approach therefore can only rely on data that is collected through correlation's questionnaires and case studies where information is obtained through participant's reports of phenomenological experiences. It is argued that because it is difficult to validate what is experienced subjectively that it is not a very scientific approach. It is argued that humanistic approach is based on groundless presuppositions, and that many of its many hypothesises are difficult to test empirically. Despite its difficulty to be tested humanistic approach can be classified as a psychology because it provides understanding of the psyche (literally soul or mind) through logos (study, knowledge, meaning). Rogers expresses his enthusiasm for a scientific approach for validating his theories when he said on page 25 of Becoming a person:

The Facts are always friendly. Every bit of evidence one can acquire, in any area, leads one that much closer to what is true.' (Rogers 1961)

One of the presuppositions of humanistic approach is that all persons are 'good' in contrast to the Freudian assertion that all humans are driven by innate physiological desires that must be suppressed by the ego, which causes neurosis (anxiety) depending on its restrictions. The humanistic approach asserts that although physiological needs are innate that they are not the fundamental motivators of human beings but rather the more general process of the Actualising tendency is. According to Humanistic perspective the actualising tendency drives a person and all other organisms including animals and vegetation to reach their potential. Rogers used the illustration of a potato to explain this point. If a potato is in a field, a perfect environment it will reach its potential by growing flowers and producing other potatoes. If the potato is left in a potato sack for several weeks it will still grow but will not be as productive because the resources of soil, moisture and sun are not available. According to humanistic psychology neurosis (anxiety) only arises in humans when environmental conditions do not supply the recourses needed for successful self-actualisation. Maslow addressed the actualising tendency all aspects of the human motivation as a process toward Self-actualisation by using a model called the hierarchy of needs. The hierarchy of needs starts from basic physical needs such as food and warmth, to safety needs followed by the need for love and belonging, which would include family and community. From the experience of love and belonging a person has their need for Esteem fulfilled and if successful is able to fulfil their cognitive needs including the desire to learn and gain understanding through education and exploration. This is followed by aesthetic needs, including appreciation of the arts and beauty resulting in Self-Actualisation. A person who is said to be a Self-Actualiser is assumed to be open to their phenomenological experience, self-accepting, spontaneous, open in their dealings with others, aware of their emotions and focused upon specific tasks, which are usually achieved. Carl Rogers added to the list that the self-actualiser would also be congruent, meaning that there is little or no dissonance between thoughts, values, beliefs and actions, with a strong *internal* locus of evaluation. An *internal* locus of evaluation is a valuing system that is based on organismic-self (Genuine Self) requiring phenomenological awareness. In contrast an *External* locus of evaluation is based upon the values and ideals of significant others which are internalised becoming a comparison for the formation of a self-concept (an image of self based on the ideals of others). According to Rogers if a person has a weak *internal* locus of evaluation then they will base all decisions upon the values of others that will result in Actualising an Ideal, which is to live by other peoples values, while ignoring personal feelings. The incongruence is a result of the two valuing systems conflicting, which causes anxiety, and lack of fulfilment. Congruence is very similar to Festingers, Cognitive Dissonance Theory that asserts that anxiety is caused when attitude and behaviour are inconsistent to one another. Jean Piaget's theory of cognitive development appears to suggest that incongruity and cognitive dissonance are a result of an unresolved cognitive conflict. Cognitive conflict is a result of receiving new information through social transmission or experience that does not fit current schema (construct of reality and the information to interact with it) causing disequilibrium. When this conflict is resolved it will lead to new learning when it has gone through a process of accommodation that adjusts the opposing schemas so that there is successful assimilation of knowledge to form new schemas and equilibrium. Although Festinger and Piaget confined their theories to the cognitive process it could be suggested that they only correlate to the humanistic view of congruence satisfactorily where Paget's description of disequilibrium is applied in a more holistic that include feelings. Fredric Pearls (1951) page 43 would agree with this point, he states in Gestalt Therapy:

The total life-process of an organism demand continual rebalancing.

Carl Rogers developed a method called the Q-Sort test for measuring incongruity (the gap between self and Ideal self) and was able to use this as a method of research to discover the effectiveness of a therapeutic environment upon congruity. A therapeutic environment according to Rogers this environment is dependent upon the provision of what he called the core conditions. The core conditions are Unconditional positive regard, accurate empathy (to be able to experience the world from the participants frame of reference) congruence or genuiness from the researcher. These types of qualities can be found in any human relationship but because these qualities were also the independent variable and needed to be consistent and controlled. To facilitate this it took place as a part of a group of case studies of participants who were also psychotherapy clients. The dependant variable was the congruence of the congruence of the participant. The congruence of the Participant was measured by the Q-sort technique at the beginning of the study that revealed the gap between self and ideal self and also after the course of therapy to see if that gap had closed. Roger's hypothesis was that after receiving the core conditions a participant's congruence would increase. This hypothesis appeared to be supported by several different researchers. Rogers asserted that the choice between developing a strong internal or external Locus of evaluation was dependent upon the quality of positive regard received unconditionally or based on the condition that ideals are adhered to in the environment where development takes place. In opposition to most other psychological perspectives which assume that food and shelter are primary needs, Rogers believed that positive regard is the primary need for all humans and that they will do almost anything in order to receive it. On this point there appears to be a disagreement between Rogers and Maslow. Maslow would put the need for positive regard in the social needs of the hierarchy of needs including the need for love and belonging, which requires the 'physiological needs' and the 'safety needs' to be fulfilled first. This disagreement is quite fundamental to the humanistic approach but experimental research on attachment from Harlow (1958) on Rheses monkeys appears in part to support Rogers assertion that positive regard is the Primary Need. Harlow wanted to see if a baby's attachment to its mother was primarily based on her provision of food, which is seen in the hierarchy of needs as a primary motivator. A baby monkey was placed with a wire-constructed mother who dispensed milk and a mother who was constructed with cloth. The monkey spent its time holding onto the cloth mother and only ventured to the wire mother when it required food. When left alone with the cloth mother and given a fright the monkey clung to the cloth mother for protection and would also use it as a safe base for exploration. However there was no comfort or attachment evident when the monkey experienced the same scenario with the wire mother. This appears to suggest that the mother is not a secondary reinforcer for food but supports rogers assertion that love and belongingness (Positive regard) are more desired than physiological needs. In relation to this study on page 115 of the Carl Rogers reader he states:

"One of the many interesting and challenging implications of this study, one seems reasonably clear. It is that no amount of direct food reward can take the place of certain perceived qualities, which the infant appears to need and desire."

However Rogers would did not accept this research as conclusive support for his hypothesis as it may not be relevant to humans and is very laboratory based. He explains on page 281 of the Carl Rogers Reader. *'I have been one of those who, over the past several decades, have pointed out the need for new models of science more appropriate to human beings.'* (Rogers 1989)

Rogers applied the effect of Positive Regard this way. If a person receives unconditional positive regard from significant adults when young, then it will be likely that they will develop high self-esteem and apply that unconditional acceptance to 'self', which will stimulate the development of self-actualisation. If a child receives positive regard on condition that behaviour is in accordance with the ideals of significant others then those ideals become internalised and behaviour altered in order to receive this primary need of positive regard strengthening an *external* locus of evaluation and incongruence. This causes anxiety when behaving or thinking in ways that contravene those ideals resulting in low self-esteem. Rogers called these internalised values 'Conditions of worth.' Freud would agree with Rogers that internalising the values of significant others were potentially damaging to a person's wellbeing. He postulated that these values would be stored in the Superego causing anxiety in the form of conscience and satisfaction when values have been adhered to from the Ego-ideal. Freud would disagree on the point that positive regard is a primary need and be more inclined to agree with Maslow that Physiological needs are primary and that social needs such as love of a mother are a secondary reinforcer to obtaining physiological needs. Vygotsky would also agree with Rogers that what is experienced in dialogue externally (inter-personally) to self becomes internal dialogue (intra-personal) which becomes a basis for consciousness or as Rogers puts it a self-concept. It is interesting to note that Vygotsky linked what is internalised socially to a person's potential development this is called the Zone of Proximal Development (ZPD). This can be compared to actualisation based upon the quality of social environment during the social needs of the hierarchy; however Vygotsky only applied this to Cognitive development whereas Maslow's theory of reaching ones potential encompassed all aspects of human development through the Hierarchy of Needs. From these examples it appears that all researchers agree that the socialisation, which is epitomised in the hierarchy of needs as a precursor to Self-actualisation, is also a significant factor in human development cognitively, emotionally, socially and behaviourally. Humanistic approach is different because it looks at the person as a whole and as a product of their experiences, while the other approaches are much more applicable to reductionism. This is because non-humanistic approaches attribute human behaviour as being caused by separate biological, cognitive and unconscious processes. A reductionist perspective implies that human's behaviour is the result of a process that controls their existence and suggests that they are not responsible for their antisocial or altruistic actions. Humanistic perspective asserts that by its nature; actualising tendency requires self-determination, and that humans are responsible for their actions, including the decision to sacrifice free will at the 'social stage' to gain 'Positive Regard.' The issue of self-determination rests on the humanistic assumption that humans are able to make their own choices in life without necessarily being guided by internalised environmental factors, as would be asserted by skinner. Skinner believed all decisions and psychological states are determined by experience and reinforcement and are predictable. The humanistic viewpoint is described by Rogers that humans are born free driven by an orgasmic valuing system which drives them toward actualisation within the boundaries of their environment. Maslow (1971) describes free will as a characteristic of the Self-actualiser transcending the opinions of others. He states on page 262-3 of the father reaches of human nature:

"Transcending the opinions of others...This means a self-determining self. It means to be able to be unpopular when this is the right thing to be. To be autonomous, self-deciding Self; ....to be not manipulatable or seducible"

Maslow indicates here that although humans are free, a transcendence of the social needs must occur before self-determination is realised. Asch, (1951) appears to support the assertion that the social need for positive regard is a powerful motivator that decreases self-determination in his study of conformity. Skinner would not dispute this finding but attribute the conformity to social reinforcement of past experience and that none conformists aren't exercising free will but have learned through reinforcement that the ethnological desire for social dominance is achieved in this type of scenario. The humanistic Perspective appears to differ fundamentally from other approaches to psychology but it could be suggested that those differences are more based upon researcher bias and philosophical attribution. This point is reinforced by the fact that studies from different psychological perspectives can be applied to humanistic approach. Its optimistic view of the individual is purely philosophical but appears provide an effective approach when applied in psychotherapy as testified by the Q-sort test.

Humanism attempts a holistic approach by addressing the parts of humans that it is difficult to test empirically and yet is experienced phenomenologicaly. It is therefore my conclusion that Humanistic approach is a valuable branch of psychology in understanding the value of attachment, self-concept and love. Alex H Parker © (2006)

Disabilities & Self-actualisation
By Alex H Parker

I have noticed that in most care and support services that the activities people with various disabilities are offered appear to focus on maintaining a sense of contentment while being sheltered form the so-called 'normal' everyday people who are separate from such services. It has been my experience that most of these services are designed to occupy disabled people only. This usually happens with minimal purpose or outcome for the individual. These services are very often limited in the activities provided and are also kept at a rigid timetable dictating what a client will be doing at a certain time. Service users must often conform to established timetables or risk losing the opportunity to take part in a minimal choice of available activities. In addition to this they are also unable to access some of the opportunities that most people take for granted such as finding socially-valued employment, or take part in an interest or hobby that is not provided by a care institute. By living an existence where choice is limited and freedom to try new experiences is suppressed, the individual is less able to self-actualise. This is because they are living in accordance with established rules where good behaviour is rewarded and behaviour that services find challenging is discouraged. This conditioning of behaviour is effective to the service because it is instilling conformity, which makes behaviour easier to manage, but it also increases dependency on the service which suppresses the individuals actualising tendency.

Carl Rogers states in becoming a person page 351

Man's tendency to actualise himself, to become his potentialities. By this I mean the directional trend which is evident in all organic and human life – the urge to expand, extend, develop, mature-the tendency to express and activate all capacities of the organism, or self. ……It is this tendency, which is of primary motivation for creativity as the organism forms new relationships to the environment in its endeavour most fully to be itself.

Over recent years there has been new philosophies introduced to care practice based on person centred approach and humanistic psychology that aim to move away from keeping clients merely occupied, but to create the conditions to empower them toward becoming self-actualised and integrated into society. These approaches encourage people with disabilities to move toward adopting a valued social role such as a job alongside people who do not have disabilities. A valued social role has been described this way:

'There *exists a high degree of consensus about what the good things in life are. To mention only a few major examples, they include home and family; friendship; being accorded dignity, respect, acceptance; a sense of belonging; an education, and the development and exercise of one's capacities; a voice in the affairs of one's community and society; opportunities to participate; a decent material standard of living; and at least normative place to live; and opportunities for work and self-support.'*

Joe Osburn Overview of social role valorisation theory which could be seen at:
http://www.srvip.org/overview_SRV_Osburn.pdf

Many of these valued social role opportunities are unavailable to people with disabilities due to the restrictions of certain care institutions. The result is that the client's may never discover their potential.

Self-concept

A major problem for clients, who have been living in a care environment such as described above, is that they develop a self-perception of being 'disabled' with all the society-imposed prejudices. They may as a result believe that they are unable to achieve a valued social role outside an artificial care setting. Carl Rogers wrote in his book 'On becoming a person.' Page 258

"It is reasonable to conclude from this study that one of the changes associated with client centred therapy is that self-perception is altered in a direction which makes the self more highly valued."

Self-perception dictates how we value our-self and what we believe we are capable of achieving. If an individual is labelled as a stereotype 'disabled person' their self-concept may become based upon these projected prejudices and become internalised by the client, resulting in a sense of devaluation. In order for a disabled client to move toward self-actualisation they would need to be helped to attain an accurate self-perception and autonomy from a care institute, and receive genuine unconditional positive regard as part of their care and support.

Unconditional positive regard

If the aim of therapy is for the client to develop a self-concept of value regarding 'self', this would be synonymous with what Carl Rogers called unconditional positive self-regard. Rogers's states on page 63 of on becoming a person:

"While he (the client) is learning to listen to himself he also becomes more acceptant of himself. As he expresses more and more of the hidden and awful aspects of himself, he finds the therapist showing unconditional positive regard for him and his feelings. Slowly he moves toward taking the same view attitude himself, accepting himself as he is, and therefore ready to move forward in the process of becoming."

This means the client must experience unconditional positive regard or be valued by a counsellor including people who run a service in order to develop self-esteem. This will have the effect that the client will not be moulded by the service but the service will be moulded around its clients assisting them to find their own individual inner resources and be assisted to become an integrated part of society. This will enable the client to accept them self as they are and develop their potential. The pattern would be as follows:

Provide unconditional positive regard (demonstrate to the client they are valued) in the form of a care manager or key worker acting in a counselling role.

The client will have the basis to have positive self-regard (value self), and act in a way that demonstrates this. This will be expressed by accepting self as a valuable member of society with equal human rights and having the same opportunities as people without disabilities. Also the belief and determination that Valued social roles are attainable.

Empathic understanding

It is the experience of many disabled people that they are pre-judged as to what their needs are based on the beliefs of others. As a result services attempt to provide them with stereotypical activities, e.g. bingo, games within a disabled institution and disabled sports, etc. They are also transported in groups to these establishments in buses marked 'Ambulance,' which further devalues them and alienates them from normal society by reinforcing the prejudices. Dave Means and Brian Thorne state in their book person centred counselling in action on page 46.

Certainly empathy communicates the counsellors understanding of the client and this fact alone might increase the clients self-esteem……………In a few cases the importance of empathy may be that it dissolves alienation, for it is almost imposable to maintain an alienated position in the face of someone who is showing you profound understanding at a very personal level.

Empathy (looking from the frame of reference of another person) is not a characteristic of society, which makes a generally sympathetic evaluation (based on their own frame of reference) of what is presented by care services, for example the groups of disabled people on an outing in an ambulance often produces a sympathetic evaluation based on pre-existing concept of what it means to be disabled. This means that a counsellor and people working in services for disabled people must develop this quality of empathy when supporting a client to become aware of their own desires and enhance the actualising tendency. Understanding the client would involve being in their frame of reference when in dialogue. The implication is that if the counsellor or support worker moves into their own frame of reference (loses empathy) if they believe that the client is attempting to go beyond what a service is willing to provide or beyond what the counsellor believes the client is capable of achieving then the client may be alienated from their actualising tendency. On page 39 of the same book it states.

Empathy is a continuing process whereby the counsellor lays aside her way of experiencing and perceiving reality, preferring to sense and respond to the experiences and perceptions of her client.

This may be difficult for a counsellor or care worker if they have a stereotypical view that all disabled people are venerable and need to be protected from Ideas that take them away from the protection of a care environment. Even if some support was needed depending on how their actualising tendency guided them, this should not stop them being able to express themselves and explore the possibilities without external evaluations. Both empathic understanding and unconditional positive regard are essential to develop an accurate self-concept. This quality is congruence.

Congruence

Congruence is a quality that a counsellor will have along with empathy and unconditional positive regard. Congruence is the sign of a fully functioning individual and without the two accompanying qualities it could be argued that a counsellor is not acting as an integrated human being and therefore is not congruent. Congruence is also the goal a client needs to achieve if they are to achieve Self actualisation. By experiencing unconditional positive regard the client will be helped to develop unconditional positive self-regard. By experiencing empathy from a counsellor the client will come to be more alert to his own experience. Congruence is a quality the counsellor displays in the relationship; if successful at the end of the relationship the client will have moved some way to developing the same quality. Congruence is explained on page 9 of learning to counsel by Jan Sutton and William Stewart as:

…The degree to which we are freely and deeply ourselves, and are able to relate to people in a sincere and non-defensive manner. For example, we may not approve of an aspect of the clients behaviour, and may aim to find a way to sensitively point this out to the client. Genuineness is the precondition for empathy and unconditional positive regard.

Effective counselling depends wholly on the degree to which the counsellor is integrated and genuine.

In order for the client to trust the counsellor the counsellor must be free from a façade that is often experienced in the care setting. This would include acting in a superior or patronising way. This will create an environment where clients can freely be themselves without feeling the need to put on a façade to please the counsellor or care worker. The result will be that the client will complement the counsellor's congruence by becoming 'congruent' also. When congruence is achieved and the client is more able to experience 'self' as they are, rather than being made to fit an imposed role.

Congruence is therefore the 'authentic self'. An individual who is authentic or congruent is more likely to develop their actualising tendency.

Hierarchy of needs

Abraham Maslow developed the hierarchy of needs, which is explained in Simply Psychology by Michael Eysenck in this way.

Physiological needs (such as those for food and water) are at the bottom of the hierarchy. Next come security and safety needs (such as curiosity and the need for understanding) and aesthetic (artistic) needs. Finally, at the top of the hierarchy, there is the need for self- actualisation (fully realising what we are capable of achieving). Maslow assumed that the higher needs will emerge only when the lower needs are more or less satisfied.

It can be generally assumed that most people including people who live with severe disability in the western world achieve their physiological needs from the state who's policies normally make available all finance and social services to fulfil this requirement. Receiving security and safety needs would involve interaction with other people who offer unconditional positive regard toward the client, empathic understanding of their individual experience, and Genuineness. When the core conditions of person centred counselling are applied in a care setting through a key worker or care manager the client will have the ground work to listen to their authentic self and explore and achieve their aesthetic needs which could lead to a hobby, education, or job of the clients own choice. In this way they achieve the goal of a valued social role i.e. student or employee. The client will then have the ability to develop their social role in whatever direction they please after becoming congruent with self, and living with increased independence from a care institution. I believe that when the core conditions of person centred approach are applied in a care relationship that psychological growth of the client will occur and an improvement will take place, however I do think there are ethical issues to examine.

Ethical issues

A service may focus upon the goals of self-actualisation and adopting a social role without using the core conditions to facilitate this. The result could be lower self-esteem for the client if they are unable to live up to conditions of worth set by a service. This would mean that all staff would need to learn and demonstrate understanding of the core qualities of person centred approach to assist the client to actualise. A care worker supporting the client would also need to do risk assessments and report any safety issues to a supervisor after informing the client, so that the client can continue to actualise in a safe environment.

Although a client with disabilities may begin to make progress there must always be support from care staff which promotes independence from institutionalised care services allowing a balanced approach to risk. It is my intention to develop the core conditions of person centred counselling to my work setting in order to empower clients and assist them to become all they can be. I will do this by offering the core conditions, and in supporting them to pursue activities that may direct them to, or assist them to maintain a valued social role and encourage humanistic, Person centred principles in training.

Alex H Parker 2003

Cross Cultural Counselling Essay
Alex H Parker

People who share the phenomena of a socio-psychological construct that includes values, beliefs and behaviours that are unique to their group can be viewed as being part of a culture. These values and beliefs can be based on race, religion, socio-economic status, gender, sexuality, employment roles, national philosophies, educational background and act as the basis of perception and subsequent behaviour. The value of culture is generally invalidated in most psychological literature and seen as a source of introjections that contributes to the suppression of the Ego. Freud (1930) believed that ethnocentric beliefs were products of the Superego and expressed as neurosis. He states:

Another point of agreement between the cultural and the individual superego is that the former, just like the latter, sets up strict ideal demands, disobedience to which is visited with 'fear of conscience'.

This assertion places culture as a source of anxiety that must be purged by a strengthened Ego to regain functioning. Freud's theories were viewed by a European culture dominated by Catholic/Christian religion as liberal and shocking with regard to the psychosexual assertions. However the theories themselves became the basis of psychoanalytic culture and were held onto by Freud uncompromisingly in the face of disagreement. Ironically, it appeared that Freud's own ideals were suppressing the faculties of Ego reality testing to the degree that he attempted to suppress further research in order to preserve the integrity of the emerging Freudian psychoanalytic culture. C.G. Jung (1961) testifies to this:

I can still recall vividly how Freud said to me, "My dear Jung, promise me never to abandon the sexual theory. That is the most essential thing of all. You see, we must make a dogma of it, an unshakable bulwark." I asked him "a bulwark against what?"

To which he replied "against the black tide of mud of ...occultism." What Freud seemed to mean by "occultism" was virtually anything that philosophy and religion, including the rising contemporary science of parapsychology, had learned about the psyche.

This example demonstrates that counselling risks breading a culture that hides behind a shroud of professionalism and implied science to form an ethnocentric truth that condemns specific cultures as irrational or neurotic. D'ardenne & Mahtani (1989) State:

Ethnocentric counsellors tend to see cultural differences as deviations from norms that they consider as global. These counsellors also presume that any differences are intrinsic to the clients and problematic, rather than a reflection of cultural contrast.

Ethnocentric perceptions are a symptom of Cultural relativism. Cultural relativism is a process of evaluation about behaviour of another person based on the cultural norms of the evaluator. For example in some cultures it is normal to wear formal clothes when attending church. Offence is felt when someone arrives wearing casual clothes, which from their culturally relative standpoint is disrespectful. On the other hand the individual in casual clothes may be offended because from his culturally relative standpoint, formal dress distracts from the point of the service.

Jung was ridiculed for his theories as they considered that parts of the psyche where instinctively attuned to culture in its many social and spiritual forms. To ignore such aspects of human nature would be to ignore the dominant modes of helping that have existed from the beginning of humanity. Tseng and Hsu (1979) asserted that spirituality, physical behaviour (dancing and exercise), medicine (doctors) and dialogue (counsellors) are modes of helping in human societies. They are separate disciplines in western society but they were once all administrated by a priest or wise man thought to have esoteric spiritual knowledge.

C.G. Jung developed the idea of collective unconscious where the instinctive and inherited resources that are common to all humans exist. These inherited instinctual resources are called archetypes and are the foundations that are further built upon by experience to create complexes that are unique to the individual but also have characteristics indigenous to the culture where these experiences occur. These contributions make up the personal unconscious, which act as the perceptive filter and source of cultural relativism.

Jung saw the aim of psychotherapy to be individuation where an individual accepts and integrates all aspects of 'self' including cultural influences and unconscious taboo's while making accommodations for incongruities. A. Stevens (1990) states:

The degree to which the self can be integrated is inevitably limited by circumstance especially by the personality, culture and relationship of the parents.

Culture here is equal in its effect on the psyche as parental influence. This puts culture firmly in the realms of superego in its effect upon an individual's level of integration. Culture by its very nature requires membership of a group who form a collective, where common constructs of reality are shared. Counselling theory is dominated by Euro-American philosophy, this philosophy advocates individualism as the ultimate expression of psychological maturity and generally ignores that there is a common collective construct amongst its advocates that would constitute a culture in its self. This collective construct is expressed through dependence on supervision groups, counselling and governing oversight of organisations like the BACP etc. It could be argued that the Counselling community suffers collective denial by failing to acknowledge the importance of group identity into a holistic theory of personality. Brazier (2003) States:

The group norms create expectations that then effect how the group collectively approach the world. This approach forms the group experience and shapes the group collective perceptions. This creates group identity and a group story about the world.

The possibility that counsellors could ignore their own secular culture, which is influenced strongly by exposure to pop-psychology etc, could present a block to entering the client's frame of reference especially if the client is from a dominantly collective culture. In addition, the client's group story may include persecution from the counsellor's ethnic origin. Resentment of such persecution could be a source of transference and prevent rapport from forming. Failure to address the cultural polar opposites can create an arena where rigid beliefs permeate to become stereotypes.

Stereotypes are always generalised and potentially misleading. Counsellors could imply a stereotype onto a person based on misapplied academic theory or experiences of people from that culture who have accessed counselling in the past. It is unhelpful to evaluate a group based on previous clients because experiences of that client cannot be representative of their culture due to the fact that most clients enter counselling because they suffer some form of distress. Making a judgment of a culture based on experiences of neurotic clients can create a stereotype within the counsellor's frame of reference, which is generalised to all individuals in its culture. Alternatively, the counsellor can become the object of a positive stereotype from a client's perspective, which is manifest as transference. For example a client once likened me to a doctor and automatically had trust in my abilities. This was a positive prejudice and facilitated the relationship. On the opposite side of stereotyping my professional role is often related by clients to internalised objects of authority such as schoolteachers and social workers. The result is that when an individual who is involved with criminal or drugs culture accesses my service that I may become a perceived object of power and criticism. This type of transference could prevent trust developing and cause anxiety to the client. Counter-transference prejudice can be felt by a counsellor toward those individuals who are involved with cultures that are viewed by society as deviant. For example people involved in drug culture may receive imitation acceptance from the counsellor who suppresses prejudice from awareness, which is aggravated by assumptions of their condition based on stereotypes. The acceptance of the client in such a situation is a façade created by a counsellor who does so to maintain their professional self-concept by expressing patronage. Such a feeling of distain toward a client hides prejudgment about the culture. This prejudgment is projected onto the client, which impedes empathy and sabotages the counselling process.

Rogers (1951) offers a solution to stereotypical perception of cultures that can lead to prejudice.

"Knowledge needs to be supplemented by experiences of living with or dealing with individuals who have been the product of cultural influence very different from those which have moulded the student."

Brazier (2003) agrees and suggests that cultural perceptions including those of the counsellor can be the product of attachment, stating:

"Meeting those who are different from our selves loosens our attachment to particular views and widens our perspectives."

Cultural attachment from the counsellor reinforces ethnocentric perceptions and blocks the ability to empathise with a client. Rogers and Brazier appear to advocate a commitment to awareness of cultures that the counsellor may encounter while at the same time examining the culture that influences the counsellor's perceptions. Much of this can be accomplished by attending workshops that are culture specific. The result of not expanding cultural knowledge is possibly a counsellor who spends too much time discussing ethical dilemmas with their supervisor. For example the western Euro-American trained counsellor is aware of the issues of attachment as researched by Ainsworth (1964) and may perceive deprivation of children based on this research. The weakness of this viewpoint is that the practitioner can develop a bias as a result.

Matsumoto (1993) states:

One of the assumptions about the nature of attachment in the United States is that secure attachment is ideal. In fact, the very choice of term that Ainsworth used to this type of attachment, and the negative terms selected to describe others, reflects this underlining bias.

Matsumoto continues to describe that traditional Japanese parents foster a strong sense of dependence in their children because this supports the cultural ideal of family loyalty. To the culturally bias counsellor this could sound like suppressing a child's independence and maturity but when we take the advice of Rogers to 'increase our knowledge of other cultures,' a counsellor may realise that some individuals are conditioned by societies where there is no welfare state that takes care of the old and infirm. The therapeutic relationship will be enhanced if the counsellor is familiar with the cultural norms but an imbalance between care for the counsellor and of the client can occur if supervisor has not received the same cultural training as the counsellor. In relation to the supervisory relationship triangle, Page & Wosket (1984) state:

Applying this principle specifically to the supervisor, it requires that she endeavour to be equitable in balancing her responsibilities towards the counsellor and the client.

It would therefore be beneficial to seek a supervisor who is either familiar with the culture of the client or who has been trained in cultural awareness. This will help to avoid pitfalls of misunderstanding cultural behaviour as pathology.

From a humanistic perspective it would be advantageous to view culture as intrinsic and a potentially healthy part of an individual. This requires the counsellor to expand their unconditional positive regard to the culture of the client in order to see from the client's frame of reference and perceive their cultural relativity. Ridley (1995) suggested five principles of multicultural competency in counselling, which generally point to the importance of accepting that the client possesses a unique frame of reference within their cultural perspective. He recommended twelve steps for a counsellor's cultural competency. These steps can be summarised as an expansion of the core conditions to encompass the culture of the client and for the counsellor to acknowledge cultural naivety to the client. Awareness of bias in counselling theories and commitment to incorporating cultural considerations into ones practice is asserted to be useful to building a therapeutic environment from a transcultural perspective. The individual is assumed by humanistic perspective to be an organism that is in a constant state of growth driven by the actualising tendency, which allows personal development, based on the quality of its social environment. The difference between the authentic-self and ideal-self is determined by the accuracy of Self-concept relative to organismic awareness. The Ideal-self is a product of introjections, which determine the conditions of self-acceptance and the conditions for evaluating others. A strong Ideal-self acts as an external locus of evaluation that uses the products of social and cultural influence as a template of reality. When phenomenological data contradicts personal perception of ideals from cultural reality then anxiety is experienced. The incongruity requires revaluation of ideal-self, which must be accommodated within the boundaries of phenomenological data to reduce anxiety and restore emotional equilibrium. The theory does not condemn culture or socialisation but rather the degree of introjected authoritarian values that emphasises cultural and social conditioning as an evaluation of self-worth. To use a religious example Christianity has an ambiguous reputation for both authoritarianism and liberalism depending on the preference of the religious instruction. An individual can either form a liberal Christian attitude with healthy self-acceptance or an authoritarian attitude that suppresses self and acts as a source of anxiety. Both are attitudes that are adopted by the same cultural religion but are internalised and expressed in very opposing ways with each polar opposite viewing the other as potentially deviant or pathological. Fromm (1960) asserts that culture is a product of social grouping based on similar perceptions, which are made up of members who create their own personal object reality of its truths within the boundary of accepted social normality, he states:

For although the differences between individuals in this respect seem great, every society is characterized by a certain level of individuation beyond which the normal individual cannot go.

It would be difficult for a non-culturally aware counsellor to differentiate between culture and an individual's degree of autonomy in relation to their cultural truths and implied absolutes without previously obtaining an objective view of the culture. According to Maslow's 5-stage hierarchy model of needs culture is placed in the social needs as a precursor to self-esteem and self-actualisation. Maslow (1971) asserted that it was the quality of socialisation that dictated whether an individual self-actualises based on self-acceptance and autonomy, or actualises an ideal based on introjects. Psychological health is not achieved by rejecting culture but rather by transcending the social needs of which culture is an important part. By a process of individualtion the individual is able to use culture as a beneficial resource for personal growth, Maslow (1971) explains:

High synergy from this point of view can represent a transcending of the dichotomising, a fusion of the opposites into a single concept.

This implies that it is the perceptual arena is a system of homeostasis, which dictates an individual's development of autonomy based on the context of cultural objects within superego. This system affects the degree of ego strength while creating concepts that maintain and contribute toward equilibrium and self-evaluation. In this hypothesis transcendence is influenced by the executive strength of ego relative to superego where a single new concept is formed by accommodation of incongruities. The process of cultural learning appears to be primarily a Superego conditioning process. This conditioning process is a reaction to experiences of stimuli, subsequent consequences of stimulus, response reflexes, behaviour shaping and social modelling during development. These processes are correlated cognitively to create schemas that contribute to a construct of reality. These constructs influence perception, beliefs and subsequent behaviour. These theories of behaviour are related to the Cognitive/Behavioural perspective. Cognitive dissonance can be experienced when cultural conditioning is challenged by contradictory experience. For example I know a woman who had a feeling of panic when put in a situation where she had to share a lift with people who were of African origin. I hypothesised that her cognitive dissonance was a result of incongruence between a racially acceptant self-concept and her own introjected prejudice that existed as a result of "social learning" Bandura (1961) as the behaviour of family members who were rewarded socially for prejudice.

On further investigation it seemed that her panic was more attributable to classical conditioning as her experience of people of differing ethnic cultures had often been a source of embarrassment to her when she found that she couldn't understand their accent. She explained that her Asian doctor had twice sent her to hospital for endoscopies for an eye infection. However I later discovered that it might not have been the Dr's accent that was the problem but rather that she told him that she had a pain in her rectum rather than in her retina. This example also illustrates the difficulties of understanding meanings when communicating with a client of differing language or vocabulary. A culturally aware counsellor will understand that verbal expressions in one society can have a completely different meaning in the client's culture. If the woman who endured the painful endoscopies had been visiting a counsellor it may have been noticed that when she said pain in the rectum that she was pointing to her eye, which would indicate a non-verbal/verbal mismatch indicating that some clarification was needed. To facilitate communication some counsellors have employed the services of a translator but it has been demonstrated that meanings can be lost during this process if the translator is not familiar with the client's cultural communication style. A translator from the culture of the client would facilitate communication and clarification more accurately nonetheless using a translator from the same culture as the client could also sabotage counselling when subject matter involves cultural taboos as this could risk the translator conveying non-acceptance. The importance of understanding a client's cultural frame of reference is critical as some individuals are referred to medical practitioners and diagnosed with a mental illness unnecessarily because of insufficient understanding of cultural idiosyncrasy. Kendal & Hammmen (1995) state:

Differences in cultural background greatly shape views of normal, adaptive behaviour. Cultural experiences determine what is expected of people, and the ethnic and cultural differences shape the exposure of the person to stressors or protective environments that influence the development of disorders.

I used to work with people from the deaf community. I noticed that quite often those individuals were labelled as rude and aggressive because the sign language style is very much to the point without much emphasis on unnecessary pleasantries. Many deaf individuals became frustrated and angry because hearing people didn't understand what was being communicated to them; this intern was perceived by the service provider as challenging behaviour, who responded by introducing sanctions on the whole deaf client group. A client who is of a minority culture may avoid association with the majority culture for the above reasons and choose careers and living accommodation in close proximity to those who are perceived to have a similar cultural affinity. A client may feel restricted by this cultural dependence and be restricted as to what life choices are available within that environment. In such circumstances a client may seek counselling in order to overcome limiting beliefs that stop opportunities and resources from being accessed. For example a deaf client may lack confidence within a work place that potentially views him/her with prejudice, leading to avoidance behaviours. Awareness of cultural identity occurs in when an individual encounters other groups. Eysenck (1996) describes social identity theory this way:

In a nutshell, the key assumption of social identity theory is that how good we feel about ourselves depends on how positively we view the groups with which we identify.

Group identity is strongly linked here to self-concept. If a minority group is the object of stereotyping and prejudice then an expectation of the dominant culture could reduce the motivation of minority groups from accessing opportunities that are part of dominant culture through fear of scapegoating. Lago (2006) suggests the two models of cultural identity, which approach cultures from their dominant or subordinate cultural perspective. Both models are in five stages and begin with a naivety of ones own cultural identity and can be generalised as follows. Cultural identity is brought into awareness causing dissonance between personal identity and social identity. Equilibrium is restored when acceptance of the individual's own culture in relation to other cultures moves from an absolute truth to a more objective assessment. As a result of understanding the issues of cultural difference and accepting cultural identity a new self-concept is developed which interacts more freely in an environment where issues of cultural contact take place. It is the role of the counsellor to facilitate the client's recognition of their self-concept in relation to their cultural identity and discover any ideals that have been introjected which effect self-esteem adversely within a different cultural setting. After the client has an awareness of their own cultural nature they can address any anxiety that is the cause of cognitive dissonance when operating in an unfamiliar cultural setting. Through the provision of unconditional acceptance from the counsellor, which is amplified by the counsellors commitment to increase cultural awareness the client enters an environment where personal growth and evaluation of culture and self-concept can safely be explored without fear of condemnation. This empowers the client to develop a sense of self-determination and strengthen self-acceptance so that they can operate according to their own decided degree of cultural regulation and according to their own reality testing faculties.

I have found this subject to be of tremendous value for identifying blocks to empathy in my own practice and have become more aware of what I may represent to some of my clients. As a result of this subject I intend to concentrate more of my studies on cultural groups that I would usually avoid due to the difficulties in understanding.

Alex H Parker 2007

Counselling for Stress
Alex H Parker

Perceptual set is involved in both instinctual and learned stress responses. It is a learning system that is based on innate templates that develop through sensory experience to cultivate schemas. The schema dictates what sensory stimuli will result in arousal and will initiate a physiological response before the individual has time to reason whether the response is appropriate. Gross (1987) defines a perceptual set as:

A perceptual bias or predisposition or readiness to perceive particular features of a stimulus.

The particular features of a stimulus can be from any modality or sub-modality. Because a stress response precedes reason the post reasoning process can be inaccurate and perpetuate stress by attributing the stress response to unrelated stimuli because the information to consider all the variables is not available. This can be particularly true when the memory of trauma is suppressed from consciousness. When a memory is suppressed the non-reasoning perceptual set is still conditioned by the trauma. Recognising any one modality that was present during the initial event, such as smells and sounds, could activate the stress response.

Watson and Rayner (1920) demonstrated this in the "Case of Little Albert." Baby Albert was used as part of an experiment designed to discover how stress triggers are formed. The experimenters presented a rat to Albert and he showed natural curiosity and pleasure toward it. The experimenters then made a loud banging noise, which triggered an instinctive stress response in Albert so that he began to scream and search for his mother. After being presented with the rat and the banging noise together Albert demonstrated a stress response when faced with the rat even if the Banging noise was absent. His response was based on correlative data, which associated the rat with danger.

Within counselling a client may not be aware of their personal stress triggers, for example Albert may not remember the experiment when he is twenty and so is unable to apply reason to the activating event but still feels stress when faced with a rodent.

A stress trigger can be anything connected to perceived human needs, Albert perceived that his safety needs were threatened when presented with the rat. Maslow (1962) expanded innate needs included social needs and self-fulfilment within the innate hierarchy of needs, which could also be a contributing factor in personality traits and stress.

Explain the link between personality and stress

The social needs are also seen within the animal kingdom where two stags will become stressed as they lock horns to win a mate and the position of patriarch of the Group. In the animal kingdom the battle ends with one aggressive victor and the submission of the looser, which passively subjects himself to the patriarch. This same stress response can be seen in humans when trying to achieve recognition.

The type A-personality is described as ambitious, motivated, and hostile impatient and aggressive, constantly trying to be top of the tree and then climbing a bigger one. The result is that people around them are often the victims of their aggression and the individual is unable to rest due to the constant demands that they make of themselves. This individual is in a constantly aroused state with the physical symptoms of stress present much of the time. This constant state of arousal puts strain on the other physiological functions such as the heart and circulatory system causing increased chance of heart diseases and stroke but he/she also finds that illnesses increase due to a lowered immune system because physiological resources are focused elsewhere.

Alternatively a passive individual still suffers stress but withdraws from the situation or attempts to placate all individuals by conforming to their perceived demands. The result can be someone who experiences stress when a request is made of them because their passivity will not allow them to say no. The consequence can be an individual who is exhausted or depressed. Seligman (1996) demonstrated that passivity might become a characteristic of depressed individuals as a result of conditioning. He induced depression and passivity in dogs by putting them into a locked cage where they received an electric shock. Their instinct to escape became active but it was frustrated by their confinement. Eventually the dogs accepted the electric shock and after a prolonged experiment no longer attempted to escape. The cages were eventually opened but it was found that the dogs remained in their passive state and made no attempt to remedy their distress. This behaviour is termed 'Learned Helplessness.' Learned Helplessness leads to passivity and depression and is a conditioned belief that autonomous control is impossible. Often the employee who works extensive hours and doesn't take holidays will become stressed and unhappy, but not address the situation and continues the exhaustive behaviour because they feel unable to formulate and execute an assertive strategy.

Passive-aggressive individuals do not feel safe enough to openly express aggression but use manipulation and distorted language such as sarcasm or sabotage. For example an employee who is disgruntled might safely spit into his boss's coffee or stick a potato up his car exhaust, these individuals feel stress, which is relieved by mild to severe antisocial behaviour.

Assertive individuals will express themselves genuinely while respecting the rights of others. When combined with rehearsal this approach is advocated as a good training technique for avoiding stress, however I have noticed that people adopt different levels of coping depending on the perceived safety of the environment and their social role. For example an assertive manager could also be a passive husband or an aggressive father.

When 'Little Albert' became an adult he may have found that his fear of rats wasn't the only fear conditioned by the experiment but he could have unconsciously remembered the experimenter who handed him the rat during the experiment. Albert could generalise his stress response that is set to the modalities that cognitively represent the experimenters and projected his fear onto similar individuals he meets in the future such as dentists and doctors. This type of transference might be manageable if these professionals are visited infrequently but if Albert found a job as a hospital porter for example he could express his feelings of stress as a panic attack when speaking to the head surgeon and adapt to the automatic stress response by becoming very passive and depressed (learned helplessness).

Personal Belief System

Albert's automatic transference could represent the existence of a core belief that is a guide to all behaviour and feelings of stress. His experience of the experimenters could have left him with a belief regarding authority figures and a subsequent self-concept, which is reinforced by unexplainable automatic panic. The belief is based on experience and becomes a schema of absolute truth to Albert.

Mcquaid & Carmona (2004) p 50 State:

Core beliefs are developed at a young age, usually in a child's effort to organize their world based upon how people around them are responding... These beliefs are so integral to the fibres of your being that you perceive them to be absolute truth.

One absolute truth that is accepted, as common sense is that the sun is bright, however if an individual applies the same acceptance of truth to an introjected value system then stress is experienced when experience contradicts the accepted facts. In order avoid anxiety caused by dissonance the individual needs take a hypothetical view of their beliefs and be open to making accommodation for experience.

An individual may show signs of stress when in the presence of a superior due to transference, and adapt their behaviour automatically to a subordinate approach. Therefore the core belief may be 'I'm not good enough.' However this core belief may be based on a ruling assumption such as "I must be perfect if I am to be respected." The assumption in tern leads to a negative automatic thought, "he is disappointed with my work."

The negative automatic thought is based on the assumption, which is driven by the Negative belief. Williams (1993) p113:

The ultimate negative belief runs most people's life and is the cause of much of their stress. Ironically it is never true. It is simply a belief, established very early in life, that the person has come to accept as true.

Accepting something as simply a belief is difficult when assumptions are the filter of perception. The information-processing model lists all or nothing thinking, mind reading, labelling self or other rather than labelling the behaviour, jumping to conclusions and emotional reasoning as non-evidence based conclusiveness.

Analyse the implication for counselling.

When people access counselling for stress they maybe in an aroused state on entering the counselling room which will reduce their reality testing abilities. Griffin and Tyrrell (2003) p199 state:

It's impossible to communicate normally with people who are too highly aroused. This is because in their aroused state they cannot process data contradictory to their black and white thinking. They cannot give attention to another viewpoint.

During extreme stress especially traumatic events the relatively long process of ego-reality testing is suspended so that innate and conditioned reflexes of the unconscious can provide instant preservation strategies. Good counselling will concentrate first of all on lowering the client's arousal through relaxation techniques before continuing the session. This helps to avoid emotionally negative thinking based on feelings stress rather than objective reasoning.

Gilbert (1998) p93 States:

When we use feelings to do the work of our rational minds, we are libel to get into trouble. The strength of our feelings is not a good guide to reality or accuracy.

To allow an individual to continue a counselling session while aroused and entranced in negatively polarised thinking could actually perpetuate stress and remove therapeutic value. Therefore it could be that a stressed individual could leave a counselling session suicidal if the counsellor allowed the individual to go more deeply into their negative thinking by revisiting all the activating events without offering any therapeutic strategy. To be aware of feelings without assumptions prevent the accompanying negative thoughts.

Mcquaid & Carmona p12 (2004) state:

This quality of mind is usually referred to as "non judgmental awareness." Non-judgemental awareness does not mean that you cease to have judgmental thoughts. Rather, you begin to learn to question whether those judgments are indeed facts.

This can be accomplished by encouraging a client to use a stress diary to record the activating event and the accompanying thoughts and feelings.

Another factor that can be included in a stress diary diet. Including a record of what is consumed before feelings of stress can be an indicator of sensitivity to that particular food. Stimulants such as caffeine and alcohol for example can have a dramatic effect on the sensations of stress. Addictions to certain substances can also trigger a stress response during withdrawal. The diary may also indicate that the individual does very little exercise. Experiences of pain for whatever reason can be a source of stress and lead to depression if remedies are ineffective.

Referrals to specialists in these fields can be effective if the individual is not able to regulate pain or diet themselves.

I feel that stress is an issue that is present in most individuals who seek counselling and therefore having a holistic approach to its causes is essential.

Alex H Parker ☐ 2007

Alex H Parker

Psychoanalysis
Alex H Parker

Freud viewed the human psyche as something primarily driven by unconscious and instinctive drives (to eat, procreate etc) these drives motivate both animals and humans to fulfil these drives. This is called wish fulfilment. These drives are instinctive; they exist without logic or verbal explanation and manifest themselves in symbol through dreams, fantasies and random thought patterns (Freud called these thought patterns free association) or through behaviour and psychosomatic symptoms (physical symptoms caused by the mind).

Freud believed that it was the unconscious drives that motivated behaviour and that neurosis (anxiety disorders) could be explained by analysing these manifestations.

Freud uses the illustration of an artist to explain this point in The Freud reader page 39:

His creations, works of art, were the imaginary satisfactions of unconscious wishes, just as dreams are; and like them they were in the nature of compromises, since they too were forced to avoid any open conflict with the forces of repression.

Here the artist is seen as expressing wish fulfilment through art and so is conscious of the drives of the unconsciousness and is in theory free of neurosis.

The artist is described as having no conflict between the conscious and unconscious and thus avoids what he called repression. The process of repression is described in Freud's structure of personality.

Structure of personality.

Wish fulfilment is an expression of what Freud called the pleasure principle, which is the instinctive drive to obtain satisfaction. He called this aspect of self the Id (Latin for 'it').

The Id is rather like a stray dog that will procreate, defecate, kill and eat without being concerned for the consequences. A human child is an example of Id because as a need becomes apparent such as hunger it will scream whether it's lunchtime or three in the morning. Id has no conscience or altruistic tendencies. So the dilemma may occur where the child wants to eat his brother's crisps and finds that because of which he becomes the victim of pain as he is pushed over.

In order to balance the consequences, a process comparable to exchange theory takes place internally between each structure. This process protects the Id from pain while providing the best possible pleasure. This assessment takes place in the Ego part of personality.

There are times when the ego must adapt behaviour to protect the Id, which results in neurosis. A person may have been brought up in a very authoritarian environment where the desires of the Id receive punishment which the ego adapts behaviour to and develops the Superego. The Superego comprises of the Ego-Ideal which consists of internalised Values and beliefs from authority figures which provides rewards in the form of self esteem etc. when those Ideals are adhered to and the Conscience which causes feelings of anxiety when those Ideals are not upheld.

If a person's drive to find pleasure is causing displeasure due to chastisement then the Ego will adapt behaviour by repressing those desires into unconsciousness. If in a future time the source of those ideals (parents) are no longer available to chastise the individual the adaptive behaviour will continue due to those Ideals being a part of the Superego which controls behaviour by causing anxiety through the conscience.

It is through the repressed reasons for the adaptive and neurotic behaviour coming into consciousness that a re-examination of those internalised ideals can be re-examined by the ego so that the desires of the Id can become more acceptable to conscience, reducing or eliminating an anxiety effect when those ideals are contravened.

Repression can hide the reason for anxiety but not the symptoms. This fact is demonstrated with what Freud called Transference. This is a process were the reactions that a person has toward one person is projected onto someone or something else. For example a person may have a reaction of panic every time they are speaking to their boss, this could be because the boss reminds the individual on an unconscious affective level of a cruel authoritarian school teacher who had impossible ideals that that the Ego could not adapt to. The only escape for him, as a child was fight or run away. The anxiety he feels is caused by the adrenalin his unconscious reaction has provided to escape, however the individual is in no danger and their reaction is neurotic. Freud suggested this process for explaining the phobia a boy named 'little Hans' had of horses. Freud explained that the horse reminded little hands of his farther because various physical similarities and so transferred the feelings of fear he had for his father onto the horse. Freud suggested that the phobia of horses could be weekend if the father began to be kinder to his son. Although this sounds daft, it is a very similar theory of generalization proposed by behavioural Psychologists, Watson and Rayner (1920). They presented a Baby called Albert with a white rat and allowed him to pet it. The experimenters then accompanied the presentation of the rat with a loud banging noise, which startled Albert, and he became distressed. After a number of consistent presentations with the loud noise, Albert showed signs of anxiety when just seeing the rat. They discovered that once a phobia had been induced that a process of Generalization took place when anything that reminded Albert of the rat appeared such as a fur coat etc. what Freud proposed with Hans was consistent with behavioural theory. If Hans father changed his attitude to his son then his feelings of anxiety would no longer be consistent with his experience and so phobic reaction would become Extinct.

Freud developed free association as a way of accessing the unconscious through Parapraxis (slip of the tongue). This is a method of allowing the individual to speak of anything at random that comes to mind that will manifest things of the unconscious in the same way a daydream is random and possibly instinctive in origin. Carl. G. Jung used a similar method called word association where a person will be presented with a word and expected to say the first thing that comes to mind. He explained its process in the his book Analytical Psychology, he states:

You ask a simple word that a child can answer and a highly intelligent person cannot reply. Why? That word has hit on what I call a complex, a conglomeration of psychic contents characterized by a peculiar or perhaps painful feeling tone, something that is usually hidden from sight…. For instance somebody with a money complex will be hit when you say: 'to buy', 'to pay,' or 'money'. That is a disturbance of reaction.

A complex is a part of self that a person represses into the unconscious due to it being incompatible with the ego ideal and is at risks of causing pain to the Id if brought into awareness. A person may have developed psychological defences to protect the Id from the painful awareness. If during a word or free association test a person pauses or expresses a parapraxis then this may be an indicator of a defence and complex that can be further examined to bring the unconscious in to consciousness.

Freud hypothesized that when something in the unconscious that has been repressed comes into consciousness that an outpouring of emotion would naturally occur, this is called a catharsis. It is after catharsis that the ego part of personality which suppressed these emotions as a child is then able to reassess those reasons a mature adult and individuate or develop those parts of personality that have been neglected and caused neurosis.

Freud believed that neurosis was caused by disturbances in a Childs development.

Child development is driven by the libido (energy). Freud believed that the libido was sexual but other researchers feel although this is a motivating factor that Freud over emphasised this aspect of the human psyche. Freud called these stages the psychosexual stages of development and that could be identified as the point of origin for neurosis.

These stages focus on parts of the body as a means of forming ideas of the world and ideas of self-driven by the Id's desire for pleasure and disruption in the form of over indulgence or neglect of the stage these stages results in Fixation.

Fixation is a word used to describe a person's behaviour in adult hood characterised by the stage where the disruption takes place.

The oral stage starts at birth. The Id derives pleasure from the mouth through sucking because it is through this process that food is derived and hunger pain is avoided. According to Freud people who experiences fixation from this stage due to inadequate nursing will be pessimistic, jealous, suspicious and sarcastic. However if a child is excessively nursed the characteristic will be a person who is optimistic and admires others to excess.

According to Freud the Anal stage begins at one and a half years old to two years. It is at this tie that the child experiences the social pressure of toilet training. Id finds Pleasure in expelling faeces. At this point the Ego's protection of Id's interests causes the beginning of assimilations of social values into the Superego.

A person who is messy, careless with a generally defiant attitude toward authority is seen as having an Anal compulsive fixation, developed as a result of a struggle between the wishes of the Childs Id and the wishes of the parents. As a child this struggle may have manifest as excreting before or just after being encouraged to use a potty.

Anal-retentive fixation is a result of strict parents regarding toilet training which the ego assesses there is greater pleasure to the Id if faeces is stored in the bowel rather than risk punishment. The adult will grow to be mean, stubborn, neat, careful and manipulative.

The anal stage seriously affects attitudes to authority in later life that could be expressed through Transference.

The Phallic stage is the most criticised of Freud's theories. It occurs from the age of three to five years old and is the stage where a child forms their sexual identity. This occurs through 'romantic' fascination with the opposite sex parent who the child wishes to have total affection from. In boys the Oedipus complex manifests its self as feelings of jealousy and fear toward the father who possesses the mother, in order to attract the mother the boy models himself on his father and develops a male sexual identity. The Electra complex is similar where the girl becomes 'romantically' fascinated by her father. Her fascination is caused by the fact that he has a penis and she doesn't and is attracted to him. This creates conflict with her mother with whom she identifies and models herself on in order to please her father.

The Oedipus and Electra complex do not take into account one parent families or cultures where the women are the dominant or equal in relation to men. Freud's theories where all the results of case studies of adults, mainly Victorian middle class women who don't represent society in general. Also much of his theories in Oedipus complex were based on subjectivism.

Freud believed that fixation at this stage is characterised by eccentric sexual expression and gender confusion.

The Latency period takes place from age five to puberty; it is a point in development when satisfaction is not focused upon any particular part of the body. Libidinal energy is used in the development of other interests such as sport and development of same sex friendships.

The final stage is the Genital stage where pleasure from the genital area is powerfully demanded by the Id, which must be controlled by Ego. This happens from puberty until adulthood. Depending upon whether there is a fixation in the phallic stage, normally attention will be given to the opposite sex, as they are the primary objects of satisfaction to the Id.

Psychoanalysis had its roots with Sigmund Freud but was developed and refined by other researchers such as Anna Freud, C.G. Jung and Melanie Klein and has had influence on the development of other psychological perspectives. Variations of the structure of personality can be seen in the development of Eric Bern's Transactional Analysis.

Observations of defence mechanisms are significant even in Humanistic Psychotherapies, however unlike humanistic perspective the Psychoanalytical approach de-emphasises the role of the environment in the formation of personality and over emphasises sexual instincts and the unconscious.

Unlike Cognitive/behavioural perspective, Psychoanalytical approach has difficulty explaining neurosis that is acquired in adulthood and in conscious awareness such as phobias and other stress disorders after a traumatic incident. As already mentioned above the scientific method for validating theories was inadequate especially his theories of dreams and psychosexuality. Freud's theories have been alleged to have been validated by his success with patients, however because there are so many environmental variables involved in therapy it is too difficult to quantify each one as to conclude which was the therapeutic ingredient. Freud was always very biased and dogmatic when it came to his theories that any theory or data that appeared to contradict his theories was dismissed and neurosis attributed by Freud to the researcher which pushed his theories more into the category of philosophy than science.

As a philosophy it has stood up to the test of time and is the basis for most approaches to psychotherapy.

Alex H Parker (2005)

Learning Statement: Non-Acceptance
Alex H Parker

I approached the course with the self-image that I am acceptant of other people's views, and value their individuality. I discovered when I was the listener during sessions, that I would be struggling to keep the speaker talking, and that I would be firing questions in an unconscious attempt to get them to come to a conclusion that was in line with my opinions of acceptable and unacceptable. Through studies of 'Person Centred Approach,' I came to the conclusion that I move to my own 'frame of reference' when my personal values and beliefs are challenged. By losing the speaker's 'frame of reference' I was unable to experience their inner world, and so lost the ability to 'empathically respond.' 'Unconditional positive regard,' became impossible, as I would interrogate the client to conform to 'conditions of worth.' I began to concentrate on developing the 'core conditions' and 'reflecting skills,' which assisted me to maintain the clients 'frame of reference' and enjoy experiencing the world from their perspective. During further sessions I have found that by experiencing others beliefs and values, that I have been able to develop my own value system and grow as a person. This has helped me understand the value of the counselling relationship, for the counsellor as well as the client. Although I have been fascinated by such theories as 'transactional analysis,' I have come to the opinion that a person 'centred approach' is fundamental to good counselling and without it very little growth can take place. The value of the 'counselling relationship,' has helped me to realise the importance of relationships in all aspects of life. I have come to the conclusion that 'facilitative relationships' in general assist an individual to mature and develop a well-adjusted personality. I have begun to apply this philosophy in approach to my son's development as a person, to assist him to feel safe enough to mature and develop, without being restricted by 'conditions of worth.'

Alex H Parker 2003

Personal Development Statement: Transference

Alex H Parker

I had become aware at the end of the Certificate course that transference is a very prominent part of how I assess people on first meeting them. I became conscious that there are people that I meet that I can have an emotional reaction to because they remind me in some small or large way of someone I have known in the past. During the certificate course it was my privilege to work with a gentleman for whom I had an instant dislike, because he reminded me of my old neighbour. When I became aware of the transference I found that I was able to work with him without prejudice, by allowing the feelings to exist and being aware that they were just caused by irrelevant comparisons, and experienced them weaken as I got to know him better.

After this experience I decided to become aware of all my interactions with finding that I was experiencing both negative and positive Transference with almost all people I encounter being able to Identify a feeling I had toward them based on very little information. I took time with each individual experience to reflect and identify the true object of those projected feelings from my past. I found this reflective exercise worrying because it appeared that I have a system of assessing people relying on my past encounters and feelings. As I knew that I was soon to start a more intensive course on the HNC, I was anxious that I did not let this interfere with my ability to take the counselling role in skills practice. But there was another problem that I was even more anxious about when entering a new class. I was now aware that I could be emotionally crippled by people with whom I experience a 'transference' that causes tremendous fear to the point of panic. I was already aware that in social situations on occasion I had suffered mild panic attacks in the past that I had attempted to hide but the fear even before entering a new class brought home to me a common characteristic 'trigger' The characteristic trigger is communicating with people who are academically successful. I would be in a higher level course that I felt that there was a good chance that I would be out of my intellectual league. I decided to trace this feeling of panic back in time and Identify on a time line where the feeling of panic had occurred in the past in the hope that I would find its origin. It was quite an easy exercise starting with bulling from a schoolteacher at the age of eight because I was having difficulties developing literacy and numeracy skills. This attitude was adopted by successive teachers up to the age of 10 when I developed great feelings of anxiety which resulted in fainting. Further in my timeline I found that whenever I was in a social situation or work situation with persons that have achieved outstanding academic success that the feelings of panic would return with vigour. This reaction was reinforced at the age of twenty two I was given an IQ test at work by a manager who was fresh out of university. The results were so poor that she felt compelled to call me to her office and give me a months' notice that I was to loose my job, I was only saved when other workers protested. The fear was present when I would attend meetings at work because I was aware of the intellectual superiority of the people there. It affected me to the point where I would find excuses not to attend. I found that when I started a new job that the same feelings were not present. This is perhaps because I didn't view my colleagues as intellectually threatening. On the first day of the HNC I was assessing my emotional reaction to the other students to see if there was the presence of transference that I could have the opportunity address. I was not disappointed. It was as if the whole class was a sea of transference, I was able to be aware of the fact I was judging everyone by my past experience with a similar other. This pleased me because it meant that I would have plenty for my journal and would create challenges for maintaining the core conditions.

There was one student that caused this same fear that had caused so much anxiety in the past. I spoke to this student briefly on becoming acquainted but although it was only a few words I had immediate symptoms of a panic attack. In this person I was aware that I was projecting feelings of fear and embarrassment I had toward the school teachers and all those who reinforced there attitude, upon this poor innocent student who in my own mind was is very academic and successful. The challenges to my development in the course were simple, can I offer this person total acceptance and unconditional positive regard? Can I get into the frame of reference and achieve empathy with someone who I am in fear of? And will I be defensive with this person when I work as the client? I decided that all of this was dependant on my own quality of congruence. I decided that trying to hide my fear would be counter-productive, as it would require a façade. So I decided I would engage this person in conversation during lunchtime and attempt to dispel any stereotype that had reinforced my involuntary reaction. I knew from my experience with the gentleman on my certificate level that by just being aware of the cause of the transference that it lost its power to prevent me from providing the core conditions, I hoped this would be the same, but it wasn't. The two situations were different. On the certificate level I had a negative perception of the Gentleman being similar to my neighbour so I had trouble offering acceptance. On the HNC class my panic was caused by the fear of 'conditions of worth' and the expectation of attack and the physical response to flee. I believe that gradually getting to know this student over time and using immediacy when I feel this way so that I don't appear rude or defensive can only tackle this. Through this approach, hopefully a 'systematic desensitisation' can occur. I do see humour in this situation because the significant others in my life who contributed to this 'social phobia' would probably see my avoidance of associating with people with above average intelligence as justifying their actions toward me maybe its self-fulfilling prophecy. This experience led me to examine the effect that conditions of worth have upon my existence and I found my conclusion was astonishing and may explain why I look for positive and negative transference in people I meet. I thrive and constantly look for people who have strong conditions of worth that I can live up to in order to gain 'Positive regard. On reflection I have found that positive regard is something I have craved but have found that I have only found its source to be conditional. Unfortunately everyone's values and beliefs are different and so it is impossible to get positive regard from different sources for the same reasons. I therefore have found myself split on many occasions as to what action is right and wrong. Despite this, as a result of the counselling courses, I have developed a stronger internal locus of evaluation when it comes to ethical behaviour. The results have been interesting.

Alex H Parker 2004

Personal Development Statement: Gestalt

Alex H Parker

The principle thing that I have learned from Gestalt theory is a respect for other people's experience of reality, and the realisation that my view if reality and perception in general rests on a weak basis because it is constantly changing with each new experience. I often found that when I took interest in something or someone it was because the subject matter was related to current Gestalts that acted as a perceptual-set, corresponding to my own current meanings. This view was reinforced after studying how the mind applies meaning to ambiguity and creates further transcendental basis for perception. I concluded that virtually any view of reality was possible, all of which were equally valid with the potential to lead to equilibrium or neurosis. During our studies of Gestalt I was attempting to formulate a new basis for applying meaning to myself and the environment because previous transcendental deductions had failed to be effective for me personally and when I was in the role of counsellor. These deductions also contradicted experience, which lead to incongruence and feelings of great anxiety due to empirical/rational conflict. I began to re-evaluate previous dogmatic, existential schema and found myself becoming more liberal in my opinions and began going through a 'cycle of awareness' that I have come to believe will be ongoing throughout life. I decided that equilibrium could only occur when acceptance of the unknowableness of the noumenalogical and the experience of the phenomenological results in an interpretation of reality that is open to further change. The values and beliefs that accompanied my previously adopted existential Schema became more liberalised as I became open to change. I found myself more phenomenologicaly aware of anxiety when faced with a challenge to previous values and beliefs and was able to make decisions and judgements based upon a more effective organismic valuing system, which appears to have replaced the external locus of evaluation through the gestalt 'principle of closure.' I came to the conclusion that these Values and beliefs were the result of confluence that I had actively established in order to gain acceptance from peers which existed in my contact boundary as a block to acceptance when those values and beliefs were not lived out by others. Although this all appears chaotic, I currently believe that I have become more acceptant of my own empirical limitations and aware of the existential human tendency in others. I am more able to be acceptant of these needs in potential clients strengthening my willingness to experience the world of a client as if it were my own without the distractions of my contact boundary which often moved me to my own 'frame of reference, blocking empathy. I feel Gestalt approach required discipline as in many of the experiments I was very tempted to offer an interpretation of what I felt the clients meaning was. I also had to resist the temptation of putting too much of my own interpretation on their body language etc. and attributing it as an indicator of defence mechanisms. However this insight only occurred to me after I was counselled and someone attributed defence mechanisms to me that I emphatically felt was inaccurate. From this experience I realised that my own interpretations constituted a dogmatic and judgmental approach and acted as a 'principle of closure' which applied meanings to something kinaesthetic based on my own 'frame of reference.' I feel it is best to allow the client make their own interpretations and that I am more effective when I only draw their attention to things that maybe relevant while having the humility to accept the opinion that they are not significant at all. I would apply this thought to the gestalt view of dreams because it assumes that all aspects of a dream are actually aspects of the self which I feel is rather narrow and unimaginative since there are other ways the process of dreams could be explained by Gestalt theory. I personally think this is an application is no more therapeutic than other approaches to dreams. In my limited experience, the client always comes to their own conclusion of the meaning of their dream, which normally is not in line with current Gestalt theory. I feel that the Gestalt approach is only useful when used to enhance the Person Centred Approach which assists a person to rely on their own resources. Although I am aware that the gestalt approach encourages responsibility I think that on its own it could make a client overly dependent on the counsellor as some of the techniques appear esoteric until studied properly. I therefore view gestalt as useful only when handled sparingly and have become more enamoured by the Person Centred Approach as a credible and effective guide to achieving Congruence.

Alex H Parker (2005)

Personal Development Statement During crisis
Alex H Parker

This Personal development statement was written during tremendous stress, and I didn't cope very well. My wife was in hospital at the time and I managed my overwhelming emotions by attempting to intellectualise them out of my experience. As I sat by her bed I found myself reading Kant. It's either my greatest work or the work of a man on the edge. The following is a personal statement was written as I danced around my emotions as if they are not really there like a philosopher with psychosis.

I have thought often during this term about truth. Truth to me is important in counselling because it is through knowing the truth of myself that I can begin to help clients to see their own truth. I think truth is connected to genuiness but I find that genuiness is based on the ever changing moment and perception of phenomenological data, whereas truth is a constant and transcends Perception.

In class we discussed the subject of a God shaped hole, I found myself wondering what shape a God shaped hole was and was it ambiguous enough to be perceived different ways by different people. A vacuum cannot exist and so I find myself automatically trying to fill the God shaped hole with an explanation as to what it is and exactly why I am at all curious. I see the God shaped hole as a great nothingness that challenges the basis for my very existence. A hole or vacuum can only be identified if it has a parameter of perceivable existence. The perceivable existence appears to me to suggest that the God shaped hole is an existential vacuum that I feel compelled to fill with perception because I cannot experience the truth that exists outside empirical understanding. I experience only empirical data and can only reason on this information to create a construct of truth that will inevitably give meaning to the confounding variables that constantly effect my perceptions and evaluate all incoming data and contribute to the formation of my Self-concept. My Self-concept is a construct that is based on experiential experience and reasoning. I feel that my Self-concept has been a source of distress for me in the workplace as I allowed myself to be badly victimised through lack of assertiveness for ten years. In my placement I found that I entered an environment that is very supportive and trusting. I have never experienced a work environment that has approached me with such enthusiasm and acceptance. I was shocked to find that this positive experience made me feel physically sick. I believe the feeling of sickness was based on the dramatic disequilibrium caused by the positive environment contradicting an uncompromising Self-concept that I had dogmatically accepted as absolute truth. As I experienced the environments constancy in its values I came to slowly accommodate this information and accept it as genuine. I came to wonder why I had become so attached to such a limiting self-concept and concluded that this may have been a defensive measure that would prepare me to be rejected. This brings me back to truth and gennuiness. I believe that truth is unobtainable and that anything that is attributed as truth is attachment to a concept as a defence against past suffering. I believe that an unconscious process created this construct and that I became responsible for its remedy when I became aware that it was not representative of reality. The reality testing mechanism of ego needed to be optimised to prevent such a construct whether positive or negative from becoming dogmatic truth. In order to strengthen my reality testing I decided to practice meditation as a means to grounding myself in the present moment and strengthen my organismic awareness. From this I have come to the conclusion that all neurosis is a result of self-concepts evaluation in relation to perception of the environment. This has been useful to me for preparing to see a client and during sessions as I am more able to differentiate interpersonal correlations that lead to confluence and inhibit empathy. As we considered compassion in class I thought about how my attachment was a protection based on the dangers I believed existed in the environment and how the acceptance I experienced in my placement was the ingredient that allowed me to become aware of my faulty constructs that I had mistaken for truth. I came to the conclusion that compassion is expressed in the acts of unconditional acceptance. It is interesting to note that it was through experiencing acceptance in my work environment that facilitated me to enhance my genuiness and empathy. I view the real truth of myself to be like the god shaped hole, an ambiguous fluid reality that can only be partially known by examination of the present moment and is examined by a limited and changeable perceptual set that is not representative of reality as a whole. What I have written so far has contributed partially to my view of human free will. I don't believe that humans posses free will but are rather the product of their experiences. I see all my clients as products of a faulty social environment where the quality of positive regard experienced in the past correlates to low self-esteem and neurosis of the present. When examining my development over the past two and a half years I can see a direct relationship between the quality of my social environment and the level of self-acceptance I experience. I believe that through awareness comes transcendence of the social stage of Maslow's hierarchy of needs and the strengthening of an internal locus of evaluation that will maintain a healthy view of the environment. I strongly believe that it can only be through transcendence of the social stage that a person can experience Self-Determination. It is through exercising the compassion that is encompassed in the Core Conditions that I hope to foster this in my clients and extend this to all people with whom I interact. This is not an easy task and will still take much time to practice through mindfulness but I am committed to my personal development and will patiently continue to nurture this philosophy.

As for the god shaped hole. I believe that it is in human nature to want to fill it. For many this includes becoming part of a spiritual community who share and introject the same construct of the existential vacuum. I was part of such a community and I believe I chose a strongly dogmatic and authoritarian religious group because it provided a rigid but superficial concept of the vacuum that offered a break from philosophical questioning but also caused anxiety when my reality testing rejected the introjects I was desperately trying to swallow as if the existential vacuum was an empty stomach craving for meaningful food. It is interesting that after 7 years in the church that I eventually started feeling physically sick when I read its literature or listened to a sermon. I eventually metaphorically regurgitated what was once experienced as a pleasant and medicinal existential tonic rather like the purging of a self-medicated alcoholic. I feel this was an important experience for me and highlighted the importance of the noological dimension of human nature that is spoken about by Victor Frankle. I feel that the spiritual aspect of a person is the clearest window to their experience as it is to this that their reality gravitates. I personally see myself as having no consistent truth in the environment or within myself. This takes the pressure away from life and I feel it allows me to experience compassion for others and myself as internal conditions of worth become weekend as I continue to adjust to this new schema. During this term I have found the grounding exercises and discussions about specific counselling issues invaluable to my personal development. I have felt freedom to speak and express my views without interruption or criticism. I think that this is because of the introduction of a new contract and also the introduction of tutors that are directive and focused on the group's development. I have personally found the challenges and clarifications from tutors very insightful and although I sometimes feel a little transparent to them I feel valued when I an attempt is made to understand my experiences. I have come to the conclusion that to refine my personal development that I will increase personal counselling as I think that having my experiences reflected back to me further reaffirms my developing reality testing mechanism.

Alex H Parker

Personal Development Statement: Automatic Thoughts.
Alex H Parker

Being in the moment, a reality that only I can experience is where I find peace. Using mindfulness meditation I have discovered a technique for journaling more concisely and for increased awareness of sensations that represent issues in order of importance. I have also become aware of sensations of heaviness and pressure in my head, which felt like a muscle that has been exercising too long with an abundance of thoughts. Through meditation I came to the conclusion that I was processing complicated schemas that may never find equilibrium. These schemas appeared to be unanswered questions gaps in knowledge, self-doubt and fears due to the uncertainty of the future and regrets of the past. I attended to these thoughts, recorded them and allowed them to disappear and gradually felt a peace that through practice I was able to summon when I became aware that my mind was processing these purposeless. Through the day I began to use mindfulness when driving my car and when at work and found that my tendency to daydream affected my mood greatly. My imaginings, fantasies and random thoughts could conger up both positive and painful emotions with little stimuli. The ability to be aware of these thoughts before the emotion they activated became my reality was empowering and has assisted me to have a more consistent feeling of well-being. The ability to differentiate between valueless thoughts and inspirationional ideas has been one value of writing down thoughts that invade my meditation. For example as I emptied my mind during meditation of clutter I had an image of a scene from a Harry Potter film that I didn't understand when I first saw it. In this scene Professor Dumbledor used his wand to empty his mind of thoughts, he then placed his thoughts into a bowl. When Harry looked into the bowl he saw a scene from Dumbledors past, which was powerful but not resolvable. I write the thoughts into my journal for the same purpose, I acknowledge them and promise to attend to them at an appropriate time. I interpreted this inspiration to be my unconscious correlating my present moment with a scene in a film but this inspiration only occurred when the clutter had been removed first.

I as I continued my Meditations I found that inspirations appeared more easily. I hypothesised that much of the clutter in my mind was a product of superego and the process of meditation was assisting me to strengthen ego which intern could access the products of my personal unconscious to deliver inspiration that I could understand. Many of the results of the inspirations were painful though as I came to realise that I had made decisions recently, which are totally against my philosophy in order to gain the approval of people whom I felt threatened by. In addition to this I became aware that I have subordinated myself to individuals and conformed to their decisions even though I felt that they are unethical. This was represented by a strong feeling of anger toward myself that was expressed as retroflected, passive depression, which I fuelled by attributing absolute blame onto myself for not attaining perfectly the ideals of my superiors. It felt like my ego was Gulliver overcome by the little people of Superego-lilliput. After realising I had allowed my introjections to overcome me I felt stronger and took action to address what I believed to be unethical practice and broke the bounds of the lilliputans. It was only then I had the feeling of autonomy to decide whether to stay in lilliput or go elsewhere (metaphorically speaking of course).

I enjoy attending the college and associating with my class peers but have found that I feel a much weaker emotional bond to them than I did during the past two years. I can only attribute this to an experience in our second year where I allowed myself to feel invalidated when I was strongly criticised by a small number of peers regarding my plans for the future during a PD group. It was an episode I would have liked to forget but I allow the memory of it to leave me feeling apprehensive when participating in the full group. The presences of our current tutors have assisted me to feel safer to participate because I believe they work well as facilitators during PD and have the respect of the class.

I have reduced my personal counselling because I feel that I don't need it at the moment. Last year I considered embarking on brief counselling but I managed to resolve the issues myself saving quite a bit of money. This has left me wondering, if I received counselling would I attribute the success to the counselling process or to my own ability to heal. By avoiding counselling I have concluded that I have learned a great amount about my ability to find solutions autonomously which would have been denied if I perceived the counsellor to have contributed in some way to my growth. I believe the requirement that student counsellors receive counselling to be without foundation and risks triggering emotional difficulties that are being dealt with effectively by the individual independently and in their own time. I also believe that the requirement for students who are functioning adequately to receive counselling on other courses to be unethical because this can foster dependence on future counselling, which I think the true reason that counsellors continue to access regular counselling themselves. I think this is rather like asking a student brain surgeon to have a lobotomy to make him better at his job, its just pointless and potentially damaging. However I also believe that it is essential if a counsellor believes they have a difficulty that is affecting their practice then this should be addressed immediately through counselling. I do feel very pressured to access more counselling by the group and counselling culture in general. I irritate myself when I consider this point because the only issues I can think of to bring to counselling are slight fear of the future for my career, which I feel I am planning for effectively. My irritation could be a sign of incongruence between my own organismic guidance and the need to gain my peers and tutors approval. This tendency to avoid isolation has been evident in my placement. I have at times gone seriously against my own principles in order to pacify certain superiors. It appears that my ego cynically suppressed my true feelings until I achieved my work placement hours. This ether makes me very passive or manipulative. Certainly this is not the expression of someone who has acted assertively. In other situations I have incurred the wrath of my superiors by my outspokenness so I suppose the level of safety I feel determines the level of assertiveness I am prepared to exercise.

As I write this statement I am watching my pet dog assertively eat my sausage sandwich because he thinks I'm not looking. I know that soon he will be lying submissively on his back waiting for me to exile him to the garden. I can't help thinking that I am like my dog, working on the principle that the risk of social exclusion is sometimes worth the sausage sandwich.

☐ Alex H Parker 2007

Final Personal Development Statement

Alex H Parker

As I stand on the threshold of receiving an HND I find my thoughts focused on how I am going to use it. I feel ready and mobilised to apply for new jobs and expand my business. These are exciting times for me because I have no solid expectations for the future apart from its going to be interesting. In the meantime everyone in the group is discussing endings. I keep forgetting that it represents a loss to some members. But my frame of reference is one of excitement at new opportunities and of a summer where the pressure of assignments and my placement is relieved. I intend to spend the summer relaxing with my family, climbing hills and reading books on Buddhism.

I am planning on starting my own counselling practice to keep me moderately in the counselling arena while I gradually work toward ending my placement with Escape. I do not have plans to make a fortune with these skills at the moment but rather to maintain my status with BACP until I have built up more experience.

I am very conscious that I don't want to be discouraged from my plans and feel uncomfortable speaking about my aspirations in the group as quite often have received what a perceive as discouragement regarding my credibility from a small number people from the group when I first started my placements. Discouragement frightens me because I have never had credibility before and any credibility I have gained so far feels weak. To be honest I still feel like I'm bluffing my way through at this stage because I am aware of the gaps in my knowledge, but to risk hearing the same opinion from anyone else fills me with dread. Of course this could be a symptom of projection and paranoia, but I am inclined to think that it's combined with some truth. I have noticed that when I feel uncertain I regress back to a child looking for approval and hook ether the critical parent or the nurturing parent in people depending on their inclination. As I write this I find myself wondering if I have enough personal development to be a counsellor but find comfort in the books of Irvin Yalom because he is a successful psychotherapist who celebrates and values his quirks. In saying this, the feeling of vulnerability is something I only feel when I am around people who are in the counselling profession and not with general members of the public and individuals I work with in my job. I am automatically assumed to be the professional with the uninitiated as it were. Despite having a lot to learn I believe that if I make a mistake they probably won't realise and it is this assumption that I can recover from mistakes and learn that motivates me to keep progressing.

I have been spending a lot of time writing my personal approach to counselling assignment and have found the experience very empowering. I didn't realise how much thought I had put into developing my own approach over the past three years. Allot of what I had written was based on my experience with clients but the brunt of it was based on how I have experienced my own PD. By putting all my favourite theoretical elements of counselling and psychology together I was surprised to see a new understanding of the reasoning behind my personal style.

I was conscious as I wrote that I wanted to include some spiritual beliefs but concluded that this was probably more to do with the desire to pontificate and justify my existential views. I believe that spirituality can be a stumbling block to successful counselling if it is connected to dogma. This is because dogma is absolute and rejects hypothetical thinking, and I really don't want to allow the beliefs within myself to become stagnant and fixed. I feel it would be beneficial for my clients if they were also to adopt hypothetical thinking when it comes to maladaptive thinking.

After my summer of relaxation I will probably be redeployed to a new job, will be running my own part time business and will be starting a new college course. The ending I am experiencing in class does not make me feel sad yet. But I suspect when I look back in several years' time I might feel some regret at not making more of it, but my mind is focused on the new beginning and I feel impatient to get a start.

Alex H Parker 2007.

References

Gross. R. D., (1987) Psychology the science of mind and behaviour. Hodder & Stoughton. London. p 98

Mcquade & Carmona (2004) Peaceful Mind. Harbringer Publications, inc. Oakland p 12, 50

Williams. X, (1993) Stress. Recognize and Resolve.Letts. London. p 113

Griffin & tyrrell (2003) Human Givens. HG publishing. Chalvington. P 199.

Gillbert. P, (1997) Overcoming Depression. BCA. London. p93

Bibliography

Gillbert. P, (1997) Overcoming Depression. BCA. London.

Gross. R. D., (1987) Psychology the science of mind and behaviour. Hodder & Stoughton. London. p 98

Griffin & tyrrell (2003) Human Givens. HG publishing. Chalvington. P

Maslow (1962) Toward a psychology of being Van Nostrand. London

Mcquade & Carmona (2004) Peaceful Mind. Harbringer Publications, inc. Oakland p 12, 50

Seligman (1996) Learned Helplessness: A theory of personal Control Oxford press. New York

Watson, J. B.,and Rayner, R. (1920) Conditioned Emotional Reactions. Journal of experimental Psychology. New York

Williams. X, (1993) Stress. Recognize and Resolve.Letts. London.

Bibliography 2

Ainsworth. M. D. (1964) *Patterns of attachment behaviour shown by the infant in interaction with his mother.* Merrill: Palmer.

Brazier. C. (2003). *Buddhist Psychology.* Constable & Robinson:London

Einstein. A. (1954). *Ideas and Opinions.* Souvenir Press.London.

Eynsenk. (1996) *Simply Psychology.* Psychology Press: Hove

Fromm, E. (1989) *The Fear Of Freedom.* Routledge. London.

Gay.P. (1995) *The Freud Reader.* Vintage:London

Griffin.J & Tyrell.I (2003) *Human Givens* HG Publishing. Chalvington.

Fontana Press:London.

Gross, R.D. (1987) *Psychology The Science of Mind and Behaviour.* Hodder & Stoughton:London

Hawking. S, (1988). *A brief History of Time.* Cox & Wyman Ltd, Reading.

Humphrey. R, (2003) *The relativity of Being* Amherst Publishing.

Jung, C.G. (1961) *Memories, Dreams and Reflections.* Harper & Collins. London

Rogers. C. R. (1951) *Client Centred Therapy.* Constable:London.

Stevens, A. (1990) *On Jung.* Penguin: London

Rogers ,(1989), The Carl Rogers Reader,. London constable.

Dryden (1990) Individual Therapy a handbook. Open University Press.

Board (1998) Counselling For Toads a psychological adventure, Routlege

Muriel James &Dorothy Jongward, Born to win . Addison-wesley publishing company.

Harris M.D (1967). I'm Ok – You'r Ok, Arrow

Berne (1964) Games People Play . penguin books

Stiener (1997)Acheaving Emotional Literacy Bloomsbury Publishing Plc

Berne. E (1964) *Games People Play.* Penguin. London.

Berne. E (1961) *Transactional Analysis in Psychotherapy.* Grove Press. New York

Bobes. T, & Rothman.B (1998) *Doing Couples Therapy.* .Norton & Coumpany. London

Butler.C & Joyce.V (1998) *Counselling Couples In Relationships.* Wiley. Chichester.

Dryden. W. (1985) *Marital Therapy in Britain.* Harper & Row.London

Sutton & William (2002). Learning To Counsel second edition Stewart. How to books Ltd.

Milne. 1999) Teach Yourself counselling, . Hodder Headline Plc

/

Quilliam. S (1998) *Stop Arguing Start Talking*. Vermilion. London

Rabin. C (1996) *Equal Partners Good Friends*. Routledge. London

Skinner. R & Cleese. J (1983) *Families and How to Survive Them*. Mandarin. London

Skinner. R (1995) *Family Matters*.Methuen. London

Berne. E. (1972) *What to do When Someone Says Hello*. Corgi. London p 41

Bowlby. J (1969) Attachment *Volume 1*. Pelican.Bucks. p13

Brazier. C, (2003) *Buddhist Psychology* Constable & Robinson. P 32

Klein. M. (1952) *Developments in Psychoanalysis*. Karnac Books. London p122

Polster. E (1974) Gestalt *Therapy Integrated*. Vintage. New York p 43.

Rogers. C. R. (1989) *The Carl Rogers Reader*. Constable London. p155

Steiner. C (1997) Achieving *Emotional Literacy*. Bloomsbury. London

Brazier. C, (2003) *Buddhist Psychology* Constable & Robinson. P 32

Einstein. A. (1954). *Ideas and Opinions*. Souvenir Press.London. P 232.

Hawking. S, (1988). *A brief History of Time*. Cox & Wyman Ltd, Reading. P 14.

Humphrey. R, (2003) *The relativity of Being* Amherst Publishing. P 35.